Fifty Years of

Collectible Fashion Jewelry

1925-1975

By Lillian Baker

COLLECTOR BOOKS

A Division of Schroeder Publishing Co., Inc.

The current values in this book should be used only as a guide. They are not intended to set prices, which vary from one section of the country to another. Auction prices as well as dealer prices vary greatly and are affected by condition as well as demand. Neither the Author nor the Publisher assumes responsibility for any losses that might be incurred as a result of consulting this guide.

Cover Credits

Photography: Dave Hammell

Conception and Layout: Lillian Baker

Figurines and Artifacts from the Author's Collection.

Jewelry: Lillian Baker, G.L. Antiques, Doris Gaston, Veronica Newell and Lynn Warech.

**Distributed By
"The Miller's Daughter"
9 Poplar Hill Road
Haydenville, MA 01039**

Additional copies of this book may be ordered from:

COLLECTOR BOOKS
P.O. Box 3009
Paducah, Kentucky 42002-3009

or

Lillian Baker
15237 Chanera Avenue
Alondra Park, Gardena, California 90249

@$19.95 Add $1.00 for postage and handling.

Copyright: Lillian Baker, 1986
ISBN: 0-89145-319-9

Dedication

. . . there is nothing greater and better than this -- when a husband and wife keep a household in oneness of mind, a great woe to their enemies and joy to their friends .   (Homer)

For My Husband

Table of Contents

Section I.
Unit I - Introductory Remarks 5
Unit II - Vignettes of Respected Names in the Jewelry Field 10

Section II. Includes 18
Color Plates & Descriptions
Black & White Photographs & Descriptions,
Illustrations & Descriptions
Drawings & Advertisements

Section III.
Unit I - Synopsis of the Years of Fashion Jewelry - 1925-1975 162
Unit II - Collections Featured with Plate Numbers 162
Unit III - Designers and/or Manufacturers Featured with Plate Numbers 163
Unit IV - Materials Utilized in Jewelry Making 163
Unit V - Current Manufacturers of Costume Jewelry, Manufacturers of
Plastics for the Jewelry Industry, Children's Costume Jewelry,
Enamelling Service to Jewelry Manufacturers and Other Suppliers 164

Section IV. Alphabetical Cross-Reference Index by Subject or Nomenclature,
with Plate Numbers 165

Section V. Glossary of Jewelry Items, Pronunciation of Foreign Terms and Types 166

Section VI.
Unit   I - Bibliography - References - Recommended Reading..................... 185
Units II - Credits and Acknowledgements 187

Section VII.
Unit I - An Addendum 188
Unit II - Value Guide 188

Section I

Unit I - Introductory Remarks
Unit II - Vignettes of Respected Names in the Jewelry Field

Unit I
Introductory Remarks

"True Ornamentation is of purely mental origin and consists of symbolised imagination or emotion only."
(Christopher Dresser)

No book about collectible and fashionable costume jewelry is complete without sufficient information relative to the designing and manufacturing of fashion jewelry in the United States. Recognizing this importance, the author sought assistance in gaining such information from actual designers and the manufacturers of top-flight fashionable costume jewelry. The author's purpose was to record vital facts and interesting, pertinent historical reference to be shared with readers of a first definitive work about **Collectible Fashion Jewelry**, circa 1925 through 1975 -- a fabulous fifty years of fantastic costume jewelry.

Works of scholarship require as much documentation as possible, thereby producing a reference work for collectors, archivists and historians. But without the cooperation of those in the field, it is unlikely that any information could be acquired, and no book could truly reflect the costume jewelry industry nor the creative artists whose unique designs deserve recognition and permanence in the printed media.

Thus began an earnest pursuit to gather historical and factual information about the many companies, their foundings, their designers, their trademarks or symbols and the manner of distribution in the market place. Catalogues, newspaper advertisements and other literature or sources could provide insight about periods of design and production; but nothing really substitutes for testimonials by those with long-time experience in the industry itself.

The author's project began with correspondence to over 90 designers, jobbers and manufacturers in the jewelry field. It was a complete surprise and disappointment, I must confess, to experience so few responses to inquiries, plus some actual hedging about sharing the "secrets" of the industry. It seems the jewelry industry is a closed-mouth, closed-shop entity.

Thankfully, there **were** exceptions, and these were to be found, by and large, among the "giants of the jewelry trade" -- those who are longtime true veterans and innovators of the industry. They were, without exception, cordial and receptive. And it is to them that the author owes a particular debt of gratitude. Because of their cooperation in providing background information, and an enormous amount of enthusiasm and encouragement, a task that appeared doomed from its slow beginning, began to accelerate with anticipation of the job ahead.

Through personal interview, telephone contact and letters, it became possible and plausible to discard or discount specific false rumors while confirming many truths . . . the primary truth being that jewelry designs have relied through the ages on innovative improvisations of immortal designs that quite simply refused to die on the drawing board of historical period fashions. These designs, in their many variations, were like some eternal spirit--a Phoenix rising from the ashes of timeless fashion for yet another flight into the realm of infinite imagination.

What high fashion jewelry evolved into, and what it can most pride itself upon, is the combination of all the exciting elements of design, plus the cloning of **period** designs which complement them. How else can one explain the charm of an etruscan pendant embellished with 20th Century chrome and resin? Or the stroke of free-for-all artistry, enabling fine crystal to experience wedded bliss with knighthood's *renaissance* hooded chain mail? What a delightful but prankish parody to partner **paste** with natural pearl! Unconstrained, but never truly contrived -- this is one of the many secrets of high fashion jewelry's success. Besides all this, fashion jewelry is **glamorous**!

"Glamour Girl", a product of a new age of femininity, came upon the scene despite the rage and upstaging of the feminist movement. Glamour is not, nor will it ever be *passe* or out of vogue. Glamour is a woman's way of life, and into that life a bit of fashion jewelry must fall. Perhaps the difference between a feminine woman and a feminist, is that the feminine woman enjoys being "glamorous". The glamour "glitz" has blitzed again, and again -- each lull but a recoup of the eternal forces which drive all women to battle for beauty external: the desire to be glamorous for their gladiators.

Interestingly enough, the word **glamour**, as recent as 1915, was a late arrival to the English language. The early glamour girl was "charming and fascinating". As time progressed, the term "glamour" gave rise to a new connotation meaning "an enchantress and seductress".

The term "costume jewelry" relates to COSTUME or DRESS and was truly the first ornamentation **manufactured for the masses** to complement a particular fashionable garment or "costume". Hence the name, "costume jewelry". But "high fashion" jewelry differs from mass produced costume jewelry, in that its appeal was aimed at the readers and followers of fashions depicted in the high society trend-setting periodicals, such as *Vogue* and *Harper's Baazar*. In fact, most designer pieces which have become the collectibles of today, were designed by those affiliated with the well-dressed, best-suited women of the world. Fashion jewelry was the unique accessory required to frame the overall perfect picture of the fashionably dressed woman.

In studying the makings of fine fashion jewelry, it's immediately apparent that the workmanship is no less than that given any fine piece of jewelry wrought in gold, precious gems, and ornamental gemstones. Indeed, some unique pieces challenge the eye and wit: is it or isn't it **real**.

To make high fashion jewelry affordable to the upper middle class, **fine** costume jewelry was contrived in sterling and gilt, set with gemstones and exquisitely faceted and foiled paste, imitation stones, or imported cut crystals. *Faux* gems, made of such superior pastes that its glass content required no foiling whatsoever, refracted light from facets finely cut against the tin-wheel in cottage industries centered in Bohemia. Man-made innovations in glass defied natural elements and some of these were set in today's most sought-after collectible fashion jewelry. A wide representation of these, designers and manufacturers, follow within the pages of this book.

The author believes the time for recording fine fashion jewelry, and the fashion jewelry industry

itself, is **now**. Recognition is past due. So this book is a beginning in rectifying an omission of 50 years, beginning with the tradition of high fashion jewelry revered for its heirloom quality. This jewelry is one of many industries which are part of the "passing parade".

Today's economy no longer allows hand-cast molds, intricate hand-work and finishing techniques. Mass produced costume jewelry can be affordable only if machine-stamping is accepted, and it has now received that stamp of approval in the industry and in the marketplace. The old, more costly methods are gone forever; certainly this is another reason why no reference work about vintage fashions can be truly complete without a tribute and inclusion of collectible, unique, designer high fashion costume jewelry of those 50 fabulous years of 1925 through 1975.

Many books about gold and gemstone describe decorative jewelry and its detailed manufacturing processes, "tools of the trade", its metallic contents and properties, gems and gemstones, its use of imitation, synthetic or glass jewels. This book will not belabor these several points, except to emphasize that **high fashion jewelry** does require the same infinite talent and craftsmanship and therefore deserves a course of study.

A **Bibliography** and suggested list for **additional recommended reading** are shown in a separate section of this book. It is made available to the serious collector and student. It also provides further sources about the jewelry industry both past and present.

The author seeks to make an important archival contribution by presenting vivid photographs, drawings and illustrations, featuring more than 25 private collections, representing over 80 designer/manufacturers of copyrighted **Name** pieces which idealizes the fullest concept of high fashion collectible jewelry.

However, this is not a book simply about costume jewelry in its broadest context. Rather it is a more definitive study related to the fascinating and extraordinary jewelry of **recent** decades, known as **collectible fashion jewelry**.

This jewelry, uniquely ornamental, is a notch below the honest gem set in genuine ore, but several notches **above** "costume jewelry" produced for the "trendy" masses who had just become acquainted with the jolly-good concept of a "throw-away" 20th century.

Heirlooms were, after all, for the aristocracy, but fit to be copied in lesser gems and gilt. The new "middle class" desired to own beautiful but **affordable** jewelry, and this desire was realized by its perfect timing: it came during the machine-age and the great industrial revolution. All this made possible the production of carefully executed replicas of beautiful and admired heirloom pieces.

Designer clothes for the upper class -- not the "upper crust" -- produced a group of fashion designers whose names have become legend in the fashion industry. Curiously enough, designers of high fashion jewelry, with the exception of a few who conceived **both the designs** and **produced** the product, worked for many companies and respected the same ethical code as do so-called "ghost-writers". These designers did not divulge **who** the manufacturers were, or who it was who worked "behind the scene".

Manufacturers who hired their own designers made no bones about keeping names confidential; and for very good reason. Jewelry making is an extremely competitive business, and it's not an unheard of practice to woo away a promising designer with "an offer that can't be refused". But there was also great loyalty in the industry; thus we have many designers who pledge their exclusive designs to one company for their full productive lives. Of course, secretiveness in any art or inventive field is nothing new. From time immemorial, patrons, kings and the very wealthy have hoarded fashion secrets: wig-making, tailoring, millinery, goldsmithing, gem cutting or even costume jewelry known as "high fashion".

Skilled artisans of the past had patrons. Those specially gifted people were--as history reports--kept virtually captives by their patrons. But they were treated with princely concern for his/her welfare. In days when wealth was measured by the treasure chest, hand-wrought creations in art, furniture, fabric and monuments in stone, none but nobility and those in the highest social strata were accorded such treasures.

As the class structure changed, so did measures of real wealth. The industrial revolution, no doubt, contributed most to the radical upheaval of various values. Women in all social stations, even the scrubwoman, could own a small gilded locket. **Sentimental** jewelry sent crown jewels spiralling away from every woman's dream. Instead, the town and country woman was satisfied by donning the considerable amount of mass-produced jewelry that was **affordable** and **wearable**.

The early mass-produced product was very well wrought. The expendables, so to speak, arrived with the "roarin' twenties", characterized by speed and a semblance of **dis**-order. Previous fashion trends ordinarily changed **gradually** from decade to decade. Yet the twenties raced on, gaining momentum at every turn -- racing along from season to season, sometimes in an utterly senseless, reckless so-called "sophistication" typical of that era.

This book, then, begins to consider the **high fashion** jewelry of that reckless era at its half-way mark -- 1925 -- epitomized by the Art Deco movement influencing **all** the decorative arts, no less costume jewelry.

Tinted fingernails in all vivid shades, began in 1925, and induced the acceptance of more open public display of **facial** makeup, too. Thus the so-called "civilized" society found itself on a par with cultures long labeled as "tribal". Surely the motion picture

image of desirable womanhood also influenced make-up, and "glamour". Part and parcel of the need to be "glamorous", was the projected image of a "glamorous woman" gracing the fashion plates of the day, with bodice lines dipping into exposed cleavages. Earrings hung long and sometimes brushed the bare shoulders. Bracelets circled the wrists and forearms, oftentimes covering the entire distance from wrists to elbows with a dazzling display of color, unique variations in design, mixed-media and brilliants.

Until the early 1940's, fashion jewelry contained a heavy electro-deposit of gold and silver, quite apparent in many of the collectible pieces sought after today. Unlike much of the tin-like substances manufactured in mass-produced and die-stamped costume jewelry sold at the "five and dime", there was indeed a good offering of fine high fashion accessories. These were touted in the best department stores. Jewelry purchased over **these** counters, were made to **last**. They were well designed, carefully cast, and hand-set with ornamental gemstones or marvellous colored pastes and brilliants.

A good quantity of the fine fashion jewelry made during the 1920-1930 decade, featured rhinestones set in rolled gold, gold filled or sterling mountings. When gold was taken out of circulation in 1933, lesser quantities of gold content was used in the manufacture of jewelry. Thin layers of gold, (gilt) over "pot metals", was in common usage. Electroplating was improved with patented "Gold-Tone" or "Goldtone" variations, each dependent on the immersion procedures and the gold content of the "wash" or plating process.

However, with the demand for costume jewelry continually on the rise, substitute materials, such as plastics and other compositions were often mounted in lesser metals. Rhinestones were also down-graded by some manufacturers to meet the costs of production, especially so during the depression years. But at the same time, fine manufacturers of excellent quality costume jewelry refused to lower their standards. These are the sought-after collectibles of today. Nonetheless, cheaper production was to be expected; the very nature of most costume jewelry was such that it came on a tidal wave of fashion-passion, rode the crest of short popularity, and then was swept under by either a gloomy report on Wall Street, or some other heavy headline . . . all in one day! A shining fashion could thus set with the sun.

Fashion jewelry kept up with the swiftness of communication; today's vogue could become tomorrow's fading fad. The "silent movies" and the "talkies" created a "silver screen" upon which shone the idols of Hollywood--the **stars** destined by fate to become dictators of high fashion, as had their predecessors on the legitimate stage or in the music halls.

Jewelry worn by the Silent Screen Stars, and those of the later Silver Screen, were creations copied by the thousands via mass-production manufacturing techniques. These fanciful replicas supplied "movie fans" with the vicarious pleasure of satisfying their fantasies. What a frantic pace it was, keeping up with the fashion world. How **demanding** it was to purse and person.

The Fashion World had its Coco Chanel, one of the first designers of clothing who made high fashion jewelry an integral part of her wardrobe. Fashion jewelry complemented and popularized styles as much as the new contagion of cosmetics glamourized a new hair-do. Chanel was a leader, and as with all leaders, had avid followers. Chanel was a trend-setter, coming in and out of "power" for several decades.

Everything was becoming "up-to-date" in every hamlet, town and city. With the speed of inventions -- made possible by the industrial revolution and its continuous growth -- its complexities brought a mixture of delight and dilemma. The easy, slow pace of living at the turn-of-the-century was wound up on the springboard of advanced "civilization", a word sometimes in real opposition to "culture". Seemingly hypnotized and magnetized by mechanization and machinery, nothing was worthwhile unless it accelerated onward and upward, *sans excelsior*.

Probably no other modern term describes the jewelry designs of the 1925-1935 periods known as Art Deco and Art Moderne, than does the word "streamline". All this fantastic change did come so quickly!

Ironically, "streamline" is not defined in any dictionary **prior** to 1920, and all subsequent definitions of the new-found, new-fangled term, are linked to designs with "wind resistance". All motifs, including jewelry, were closely related to those lines which permitted a velocity of SPEED to enter into the design -- be it in designing racing cars, airplanes, buildings, "streamline" and "jetstream" modes of transportation, or the new patterns in ornamentation and adornment--all flashing streaks of line imitating lightning or the speed of the phenomenon.

So came the recognizable designs in modern plastics -- designs with unhampered, unfettered, direct line in its most abstract form. "Streamlining" dictated trends toward utmost simplification, with no obstructions to impede the line. It was dominated by a single thesis, one uncomplicated by the myriad of mysterious ins-and-outs demanded by the lazy weavings and intricacies of Victorian, Edwardian and *Art Nouveau* ornaments and jeweled mountings. Those frankly maudlin settings for gemstones were enhanced by fragile mountings much like a shrine to sentimental adornment; as such, they had no place in a modern world spell-bent to rushing, with no time to "stop and smell the flowers".

Art Deco and Moderne jewelry were blatant signs of their times -- a time for precise line, clarification and coordination of color, and all on a manufacturing schedule and deadline allowing no deviation in production programming. The makers were the disciplined disciples of a market-mania.

Of course, ancient traditional designs did then and have still remained the pillars of production in all jewelry making. The artful contrivance of the basic designs and the meritorious use of man-made materials, did produce some types of jewelry recently rediscovered and reclassified as "collectible". Many of these are the unique adornments made of thermoplastics and resins. During World War II, when there were severe restrictions on tin, copper, rhodium and silver, the jewelry trade was both taxed and vexed by the challenge of producing alluring ornamental jewlery, enough to brighten those dark days of war. Much to their credit, they rose to this task by producing a newly inspired approach to fashionable costume jewelry.

Decorative costume jewelry lit up the marketplace with eye-catching, brightly colored plastics, ingeniously carved or inlaid with contrasting shades, or brightened with brilliants. These were the **newer**, more resilient plastics which took their lead from the Dadaists and Cubists, the artisan/designers of an earlier approach.

There are dozens of reference books on the subject of Art Deco and Art Moderne **design** and its **influence**, but there's a woeful lack of singular reporting on that all important personal adornment -- **jewelry**.

Research into these periods presents in the printed word, truly complex studies. Each transfers or contradicts the many engaging theories, one from another--from one author to another. The basis for many of the hypotheses set forth in these books, are often suppositional and occasionally too academic. Some are even presumptive; a few rather impractical and abstract, when one considers all the documentation and historical materials readily available in numerous archives, all related to vintage clothing, including the entire realm of the fashion industry.

Too many books about Art Deco and Art Moderne design periods tend to present historical reports of human endeavor **in all areas**, while **ignoring** what has been everlasting: personal ornamentation. The personal adornment of men and women of the 1925-1975 decades were as quakeful a jolt to design-theory, (no less mores and manners), as was the shuddering of change from cave-like existence to planetary landings. During the turbulent sixties of our 20th century, there was a movement almost aboriginal in its donning of decorative adornments consisting of shells, trade beads, fiber necklaces and bracelets. There was a noticeable absence of rings and earrings. This "hippie" trend was a relapse back into the 19th century, into a period known as the "Aesthetic Period". It had the same shunning of things "manufactured and marketed for the masses". The decade of the sixties, with its "flower children", was clearly reminiscent of these early 1900's, with its longing to return to a "serene order and simple life" of Medieval Knights and their *Faire Ladies*. This seeming "simplicity" was reflected in a return to "natural" adornment in jewelry. Unfortunately, the "hippie" contingency of young folk not only "smelled the flowers"--they smoked them. Thus the period gradually thinned out, **evaporated** so to speak, into thin air, leaving a pollution of acrid smoke rising from a chimney-pipe.

Within two decades, there evolved from this **original** Aesthetic Period, the British Arts and Crafts Movement, which eventually paved the road leading to a broadening of *Art Nouveau* -- the "new art". (The psuedo-Aesthetic Period of the 1960's, had no such illustrious progeny, having produced nothing memorable except for the **sane** production of **glamorous** costume jewelry for **"realists"**.)

The "new art" was the cornerstone evolving into the Art Deco design period. In our own 20th Century, we have witnessed yet another of the "arts and crafts" craze with a shrugging off of the "new" Space Age "technocracy", which brought the gorgeous high fashion jewelry collectibles--"glitz" and plastics, circa 1940-1950.

The artist/jewelers of the new Machine Age, though bitterly resenting at first the intrusion of the mechanical and technological "monsters", finally accepted and then joined in reaping the benefits of the more realistic and futuristic promises springboarding from the Industrial Revolution.

Machines and mass production were here to stay, and nothing influenced the art of jewelry design to a greater degree than did the arrival of those "mechanical monsters". Die-stamping superceded hand-wrought pieces, and the evolution in manufacturing and the revolution of peoples against traditional values -- both moral and material -- produced the new artists/jewelers of an exciting and truly exhilerating time. It was they who initiated a new concept of utilizing and revitalizing an artistic line so that the ingenious **machines** could be mastered and so produce an ageless beauty of its own.

Craftsmanship and design were not entirely sacrificed at the altar of progress, as is fully apparent in our day, as we witness the demand for the fashionable fine costume jewelry of the 1925-1975 yester-years.

Indeed, the demand is rising for the flow of **reproduction** jewelry made in the years spanning 1925-1965. Today's markets are being flooded, yet collectors swim ever eager with the tide, fishing for elegance of design and "name jewelry" that will be tomorrow's "collectible".

The jewelers and craftsmen of the *nouveau* period discovered a perfect intermingling of fantasy and realism, a half-escape from "progress". Theirs was an introduction into an almost hallucinated state, producing jewelry of decadent decorativeness, in a totally decadent age of Art. Although this decadence was mainly apparent in the literature and graphics of the 19th century and early 20th century, too, the perverseness of the squirming linear line in *Art Nouveau*, the geometrical cubical form of Art Deco, seemed to sacrifice the literalness of jewelry design. "Free form" swept uncontrolled into literature and art, thus producing **"poetic license"** and **"art for art's sake"** to an **extraordinary** degree.

The "new art" movement, recognized by different names in various countries, earns merit as the **beginning of artistic fabrication, an integral part of the mechanization process and progress**. Although the "new art" jewelers turned a deaf ear to technical advances of mass production, the unrelenting roar of conquering machines drowned out the protests of those who could not -- or would not -- advance with the times. Instead, those who dreamed of utopian ideas and ideals encompassing **compatibility** between "hand-made" and "mass-produced" jewelry, soon dismissed the projected nightmares foretold by the lofty followers of William Morris who had **un-prohetically** announced: **"the great intangible machine of commerical tyranny (will) oppress us all . . ."**

The final recourse for those not wishing to be part of the passing parade, was to simply design **for** those machines, and have those "monsters" eating out of ones hand -- but not be devoured in the taming.

Thus the motivation for industrial design was conceived by the very craftsmen who most feared the techniques of technology and the so-called "calamities" it would bring. What had begun as a rebellion against the Industrial Revolution, resolved itself into a peaceful though troubled existence still being argued to the present day. One thing is certain, no other group took such advantage of the "new age of technology", as did the resourceful manufacturers of fine fashion jewelry for the masses.

Then, as now, there's much imitation in jewelry design, both deliberate and coincidental. Exact copies were and are made of fashionable decorations, jewels and "conceits". Exhibitions of great jewelers' works are always a great world-wide influence, with each country not above copying "the masters" in either precious ores or gilt, with genuine gems or paste.

It's difficult even today, to attribute **unmarked** pieces to a partiuclar country or cult, no less a manufacturer. So varied are copies that only a few eccentric designers and jewelers survive in their own right. But times are changing, and the emphasis **is** shifting to recognition of individual **designers** of jewelry.

Therefore, the author trusts that the reader will find it exciting to view the photographs in this book which primarily feature **marked** pieces of high fashion jewelry, readily identified not only by a manufacturer's mark, but by the unique and definitive style of the talented designer.

9

Unit II
Vignettes of Respected Names in the Jewelry Field
Author's Note

These short monographs were not selected at random. A letter of invitation was mailed to almost 100 of the top names in the high fashion jewelry industry. It was an invitation to participate in my project, and to provide factual historical information for inclusion in this first definitive work on the subject.

Unfortunately, the majority of the jewelry houses advised me that they do not keep records, nor do they have archival material. Only in the last decade or two, have jewelry companies and manufacturers recognized the importance of keeping records. Today's technology, such as micro-filming, makes it possible for accurate records of production, photographs, advertisements, designs, sketches, and all other pertinent information relative to the industry, to be carefully preserved. The author encourages a formation of archives within the industry.

The sketches that follow can, in a sense, provide a blueprint for others involved in the fifty years of adept adaptations of jewelry making, skills, production practices and background. The vignettes herein chart only a surface course and do not, in the space allowed nor with the materials at hand, give the kind of depth such an account could have achieved had the author been granted the necessary tools of the writing craft: facts, documents, photographs, etc.

To those who did provide such information, the author trusts that her versions are of a complimentary nature, as was intended.

Perhaps this true anecdote will serve as the highest compliment:

A friend and avid jewelry buff visited a very fine jeweler in San Francisco. She asked him who his designers were, and where the ideas came from. His response was that he had no need for designers because the best ideas come from copying high fashion costume jewelry, reproducing the designs in gold and gems.

[The jewelry companies that are the subject of the vignettes, are listed **alphabetically**, and not necessarily in order of preference, personal or otherwise.]

Ciner Jewelry

*[Based on a telephone interview with
Mr. Irwin Ciner, retired]*

Emanuel Ciner founded **Ciner** jewelers who in 1892 manufactured only gold jewelry set with precious gems of the highest quality and craftsmanship.

Ciner is a family-owned company, now into its third generation. When Irwin Ciner, son of the founder, retired several years ago, the family business was taken over by his daughter, Pat, and her husband. They are in charge of operating the New York based firm.

Ciner--one of the few jewelry manufacturing companies that ventured into the early costume jewelry industry field, (1931)--always designed and copyrighted its own line using a patented gold electroplate process. **Ciner** was one of the first to recognize the need and enormous potential of good mass-produced costume jewelry. However, it took the lead in making **fine** jewelry for the high fashion market.

Prior to World War II, **Ciner** introduced sterling silver jewelry as "high fashion"; but when the war came, silver was a restricted-use metal, and like others engaged in the manufacture of costume jewelry, **Ciner** resorted to the substitute metals which could be successfully electroplated with Ciner's own patented processes.

Ciner's dies for imitation stones were made by German workers in the many "cottage industries" located in Germany and Czechoslavakia. Only Swarovski's finest rhinestones, with and without foil, were imported by **Ciner** .

In 1967, **Ciner** fashion jewelers celebrated its 75th year, with their **"precious looking"** jewelry -- one of their many favored slogans -- shown at the fine jewelry counters of Bonwit Teller, (New York & Philadelphia); Sakowitz, (Houston), and I. Magnin (on the West Coast).

Ciner was always considered **top-of-the-line**, for high fashion costume jewelry, and had the reputation of being **"The Tiffany of Costume Jewelry"**. Deservedly so.

Eisenberg Jewelry

*[From a telephone interview with
Karl S. Eisenberg, President]*

Jonas Eisenberg, one of thousands of immigrants who arrived from Austria in the late 19th century, settled in Chicago in 1880, where he opened a business offering ready-to-wear women's fashions. What made Eisenberg's fashions unique, was the jeweled accessory -- a glittering rhinestone pin -- a galaxy of sparklers that created a sensation. The gorgeous brilliance was achieved by "Strauss Austrian crystal", which Jonas Eisenberg imported from Swarovski Company, Austrian manufacturers of glass rhinestones containing exceptionally high lead content. Because of this, there was no need to use foil-backings to produce the desired brilliance and highlights. Makers of the highest quality and finest faceted rhinestones since the late 19th century, Swarovski still supplies Eisenberg Jewelry company with flawless rhinestones, including a production of faceted imitation ornamental gemstones, using foil to heighten their color and clarity.

In 1895, Karl Eisenberg's father was born, as was an uncle, and these two ambitious men continued Jonas Eisenberg's enterprise which had begun in 1914. At that time, Eisenberg's garments and jeweled accessories were contracted out to jobbers. However, in 1930, the Eisenbergs designed and manufactured their own much sought-after label: "**Eisenberg Originals**", which was sewn into the fashionable clothing. Sales franchises were sold to only the **major** department stores. In the beginning, there were 500 franchises throughout the United States, limited to one department store in each city. Only these stores were allowed to handle the exclusive ladies' fashions with the famed "**Eisenberg Originals**" label.

However, it never occurred to the Eisenbergs that they should market their early rhinestone jewelry; therefore, it was not trademarked, design-patented, or identified except for its recognized superior quality of design, mounting and settings of varied shapes of brilliant rhinestones. Because the handsome pins were continually "lifted" from the garments, one of the managers of a leading department store suggested that Jonas Eisenberg set up a facility of his own for the express purpose of selling exclusive **Eisenberg** jewelry. This he did with much success.

Early 1930 Eisenberg jewelry was simply marked "sterling", and was not stamped with the name of the maker. Then came the **Eisenberg** mark, followed by **Eisenberg Original** (with the copyright symbol). It was not until 1950, with the use of rhodium, that **Eisenberg Ice**--a name suggested by Karl Eisenberg's father-- became the much respected and sought after mark for this luxurious, artistic and most distinctive high fashion jewelry.

Around 1930, **Eisenberg Originals** came in a blue velvet box inscribed, "**Eisenberg & Sons Originals**". These pieces had mounts made of sterling.

Eisenberg Originals, around 1940, were elegant in design, but cast in pot metals due to the World War II restrictions on silver and other metals urgently required for the war-effort.

From 1950, and through the sixties, rhodium was used exclusively because of its durability and non-tarnishable qualities.

In approximately 1975, the company was more or less in limbo for almost five years. In the decade that followed, and without realizing the market potential of the **Eisenberg** name and design copyright, many major pieces of jewelry were sent out unmarked except for a tag. Too, because casting costs became prohibitive, contemporary pieces had machine-stamped mountings, but the quality of finish and the stones remained excellent, thus upholding the **Eisenberg** standards of perfection.

All stones which had been previously hand-set, were now both prong-set and/or glued. Today's glue, much improved over its crusty counterpart of yesteryear, is of such a make-up that it safely leaves the foil bright and unaffected. Space-age adhesives used on **Eisenberg Jewelry** are the same kind tested to adhere a propeller to an engine. Furthermore, the chemical compositions of the settings allow as many as 27 baked-on enameling processes to assure contrast and clean color in various designs.

One of New York's most prestigious designers, Florence Silverman, was joined by contracted artists to produce the blueprints, designs and prototypes for **Eisenberg Ice** trademarked and copyrighted jewelry. The actual manufacturing is done in Long Island, New York. **Eisenberg Jewelry** company headquarters is still in Chicago, with showrooms in New York and Los Angeles.

Advertisements of copyrighted **Eisenberg** designs appeared in leading fashion magazines in the decade of the sixties, touting slogans such as: "THE GLITTERING GENERATION MOVES UP TO EISENBERG ICE", to "reflect their own fashion and fire".

In 1967 ("the year of the ear") came the glittering glory of pendant earrings truly blazing with light, and the "**Midas Touch . . . they're either real or Eisenberg Ice**", was a well known slogan. **Eisenberg Ice** jewelry was sold in only the finest retail stores and advertised exclusively in trend-setting high fashion magazines such as *Vogue* and *Harper's Bazaar*. An interesting sidelight: in the 1940's, the Art Institute of Chicago's gift shop sold **Eisenberg** jewelry from $25-$50-$75 to $125. Considering the

WWII value of the dollar, when workers were earning as little as $10 per week, **Eisenberg** jewelry was considered, even then, a luxury and a worthy "investment". Those who purchased early **Eisenberg** pieces may well applaud such instincts, realizing much increase in value as well as market demand by serious collectors.

The **Eisenberg** story is typical of many success stories experienced by early immigrants who not only **believed** that America's sidewalks were paved in gold, but proved by their industry and ingenuity that "hard work makes one lucky", and thus "went for the gold".

Jonas Eisenberg sought opportunity in "the new world", America. He made his own legacy by personal dedication, and his legacy has been handed down to his descendants. Among them, his grandson Karl S. Eisenberg, today's head of the fine company, **Eisenberg Jewelry**.

Emmons Jewelry
and sister company Sarah Coventry

[From interviews: Elaine Dill, Mary Harrington; archival material: Valmai Monteith, Eleanor Musser, and author's collection; letter: Tom Healy; phone interview: Randy Hex]

Charles H. Stuart, founder of **Emmons** fashion jewelry company, named the exclusive jewelry sold only through "home fashion shows", after his wife, Caroline Emmons. **Sarah Coventry** jewelry received its name from the Stuart's grand-daughter. **Emmons Jewelers, Inc.**, Newark, New York, was headed by William Scheetz, President who succeeded E.F. Farrell in the late 1950's.

In the beginning, **men** put on the first "home fashion shows". One of the first was Al Wrench whose wife acted as "hostess" by inviting friends and neighbors to a get-together for the express purpose of "**learning all about Costume Jewelry, how it can be worn, how to choose what they want at popular prices, and how they can get MORE Emmons Jewelry, as Hostess Gifts**". What began in modest circumstances boomed into big business, with literally millions of American women participating in the newest rage for "home parties". It was an undeniably unusual concept of selling fine costume jewelry. The plan succeeded primarily because the product was of unusually high standard in both quality and design.

Neither **Emmons** nor **Sarah Coventry** designed or manufactured their own fashionable costume jewelry. **Emmons** and its sister company, **Sarah Coventry**, [C.H. Stuart & Co.], were strictly distributors who **bought** designs that were then manufactured by them and various other producers located in Providence, Rhode Island.

Emmons was incorporated in February 1949; **Sarah Coventry** came into being about eight months later. Emmons Jewelry Co., Inc., is now out of business, and **Coventry** jewelry is no longer sold on the "party plan" (since 1984), but is issuing fine gold and gemstone jewelry licensed under P&B Manufacturers. This last information is courtesy of Randy Hex, Director/Public Relations, for the Rhode Island based firm.

In 1952, the author became a "Fashion Show Director", for **Emmons**; within three years came a promotion to District Director. Within that time, approximately 45 women -- mostly housewives -- were hired and trained by me as **Emmon's** "Fashion Show Directors". The majority of these women sought supplemental incomes and worked evenings and weekends. Under the directorship of the author, the "enthusiasts" became the leaders in the entire Southern California District. In 1954, it achieved recognition as the "Honor District", competing on a national basis. On October 11, 1954, Lillian Baker's "Enthusiasts" were guests of Bob Crosby on his TV program. Each Fashion Show Director received a unique "Bobcat Pin", (see color Plate 6), and toured the CBS sound stages.

Instead of being competitors to the retailers of costume jewelry, **Emmons** and **Sarah Coventry** jewelry fashion shows in the home increased the sales and general interest in top quality fashionable jewelry. Hundreds of women who had previously purchased "cheaper by the dozen" jewelry pieces at corner drugstores or neighborhood "five-and-dime" enterprises, began to realize the pleasures and real longtime investment in better, fashionable, jewelry. They learned to appreciate quality, design, workmanship and the importance of wearing jeweled accessories.

Emmons' District Directors built up their organizations by urging housewives to "Brighten your living . . . Lighten your budget . . . Do something you'll enjoy!" **Fashion-Magic Jewelry** by **Emmons**, was offered as a career with many rewards. As their advertising brochures stated:

You get out regularly. You meet people and make new friends.

You will be in business for yourself. You set your own working hours that do not interfere with family.

Your family will know where you'll be at your shows -- that you will be with women, and that you'll be earning money.

You participate in exciting sales contests that enable you to add fine prizes and Awards to your earnings.

You get a whole showcase full of Emmons "Fashion-Magic" Jewelry to show and to wear -- at no cost to you.

You get a light, attractive carrying case for the jewelry.

You also receive NEW JEWELRY from time to time -- at no cost to you -- to keep your sample line bright and fashion-fresh.

You develop self-confidence and poise.

You learn how to be at ease with people you've just met.

You get good training -- to get you off to a good start and to help you get the most out of your work.

You get good pay. You earn while you learn. You start earning with your very first Show.

You do no delivering, and no collecting for deliveries.

You offer the Emmons Opportunity to friends and other fine people, and you may become one of our Key People who win extra **Awards** and Prizes, too.

AND . . . You can earn advancement to Unit Sales Leader, even to Branch Manager, with prestige and opportunity for increased earnings.

In 1962, **Emmons** printed a pamphlet outlining the "Appropriate Jewelry For These Fashion Types". The flyer is a wonderful historical "document" of its time, especially to those interested in the jeweled accessories and vintage clothing circa 1960:

Young girls to teenagers . . . . Bracelets, Necklaces, Tailored small pins or Conversation Piece Pins. [Prancer Pin, Flowerette, My Secret Necklace, Chameleon]

The Business Woman . . . . . Pin and Earring Ensembles, Bracelet & Earrings, Bibs, Chains. [Model's Choice, Siamese Charm, Harvest Glory, Fashionette]

Older Women . . . . Tailored or Dressy Conventional Necklaces and Earrings. [Circlets, Golden Braids, Sovereignty]

College and High School Gals . . . . *Sautoirs*, Chain-Type Necklaces, Pearls. [*C'est Belle*, Confection, Caprice]

Young Boys . . . . Tie Bars, Cuff Links (Small, Tailored or conversation-piece Type) [My Friend Ensemble]

Business & Professional Men; Men dressed for an evening out . . . . Tailored or Fancy Sets; Key Chains. [V.I.P. Regal, Twin-Key].

Short Women on your list . . . . Smaller Pins & Earrings; Dainty Necklaces [My Favorite, Golden Veil, Dainty Butterfly]

Tall, stately ladies . . . . . Bold Pins; Wide Bracelets; Big Earrings [Amber Glow, Flower in Filigree, Tapestry, Fashion Frost]

Grandmothers . . . . . Pins, (Fancy or Plain), conventional necklaces. [Rainbow Star, Blue Shadows, Circlets]

For the Woman who likes to entertain . . . . . Rhinestone Sets; Rings [Sovereignty Acclaim, Blue Ice]

For the Woman who wears SUITS . . . OVERBLOUSES . . . SHEATH DRESSES . . . EVENING CLOTHES . . . SWEATERS & SKIRTS . . . Emmons "prescribed" a series of named jewelry pieces, including "Waterlily", "Pansy Duet", "Elegance, "Inca Princess", "Magic Lantern", etc. [Variations of "Magic Lantern", are shown in a series of drawings distributed by EMMONS Jewelers. See page 26.]

The brochure, circulated among the "guests", concluded with gift-giving ideas, with the following statement--as true today as three decades past: **"If you're still in doubt, remember--everyone loves PEARLS!"**

Stars of stage and screen wore **Emmons** and **Sarah Coventry** jewelry and it became a popular give-away on *Queen for a Day*, and other televised programs. Hundreds of celebrities--famous men and women in many professions--wore **Emmons** and lent their name to advertising: Lois Hunt, lyric soprano; Joanie Summers, Pamela Mason, Dianne Foster, Jessie Royce Landis of New York and London stage; TV and movie stars Jayne Meadows, Gwen Verdon and all Miss America contestants from 1961 - 1965. Famous names such as Kathy Nolan, Kenny Miller, Peter Donat, Eileen Heckart, Lotte Lenya, Terry Moore, Lee Remick and Colleen Gray, joined the list.

Emmons Jewelry was worn by Academy Award Winner, Patricia Neal, and Paula Prentiss, both appearing in Otto Preminger's 1942 motion picture, *In Harm's Way*, based on a story about Pearl Harbor.

Home "jewelry fashion shows" were also hosted by very successful male counterparts as Fashion Show Directors. During the post WWII years, women didn't hesitate being out alone at night, or even arriving back home after 11:00 p.m.; but as the decades brought changes in "life-styles", it became evident that from a safety factor alone, women would be difficult to hire as Fashion Show Directors. High crime rate, unsafe neighborhoods, radical changes in mores and manners, put the padlock on the door of opportunity which **Emmons** and **Sarah Coventry** had opened to so many men and women.

Jewelry Fashion Shows are part of past history in the ever-changing story of the jewelry industry as a whole. From the author's personal viewpoint and experience, it is history worth re-telling via this volume.

Haskell Jewels, Ltd.

[Information courtesy of: Correspondence/Sanford G. Moss, Pres., Haskell Jewels, Ltd.; Telephone interviews/Malcolm H. Dubin, nephew of the late Miriam Haskell; Sharry Clark's personal interview with Mr. Moss at Haskell's New York facility; and material from Baker's archives]

Haskell Jewels, Ltd., has been producing the internationally respected name of **Miriam Haskell** jewelry, in what has remained a totally self-contained, privately owned, company. Mr. Sanford G. Moss, President, is the sole owner and only the third proprietor of a company that has been producing and selling the finest high fashion costume jewelry consistently since 1924.

Mr. Moss met the maker of the jeweler bearing her name -- Miriam Haskell -- only once, about 1955, when he joined the organization then belonging to Miriam's younger brother, Joseph Haskell.

Miss Haskell had already sold the company to Joseph Haskell in the early 1950's. Upon his retirement, the business continued in its splendid tradition under the leadership of Mr. Moss. The transfer of all holdings was effected approximately 1956. Thus, **Haskell Jewels, Ltd.**, came into existence under a new title but with ever a mindful eye on continuation of handmade jewelry ala **Miriam Haskell** of old.

It is appropriate that Mr. Moss and his wife should own **Haskell's** flourishing business. Mr. Haskell's private treasure of more than 5,000 vintage **Miriam Haskell** pieces acquired over the years, plus the wide collection of later editions in his wife's collection, tells of their early and continuing appreciation of **Miriam Haskell** designs and influence.

Today's company, **Haskell Jewels, Ltd.**, employs 65 talented people who work diligently on 22 different designs which sell to prestigious stores such as: Saks Fifth Avenue, Marshall Fields, Neiman Marcus, Bonwit Teller and various high-fashion mail order catalogue companies.

Ralph Loren recently collaborated with **Haskell Jewels, Ltd.**, in producing a piece that will be sold exclusively in conjunction with Loren's fashion. This piece designed for Mr. Loren consists of a seven-strand pearl choker-necklace with an ornately jeweled **detachable** brooch. This pin may be worn as an accent to the choker-necklace, or to highlight by itself a suit or other garment.

Each **Haskell** piece is made "the old fashion way". It's meticulously hand assembled, each bead carefully measured to match in size. Each employee works at her own pace, from inception to the finished piece. All activity takes place at **Haskell Jewels, Ltd.**, located at 200 Madison Avenue, where office and showrooms are located. This is its third location since the company was founded. Showings are by appointment and/or invitation only. As reported by Sharry Clark, following a visit to **Haskell's** facilities: "The building is indicative of the product. It gave my husband and me the impression of being inside a palace."

A "rags-to-riches" story has been related to the author by Miriam Haskell's nephew, Mr. Malcolm H. Dubin. How did Miriam Haskell first venture forth as a self-made businesswoman? Mr. Dubin suggests that she may have been financed on her first venture into her own business by her father, Simon Haskell, who owned his business at 218 State St., New Albany, Indiana.

Miriam had worked for her father as a teenager. Perhaps this was the beginning of her experience in sales work. Her mother, Rebecca Haskell, outlived Simon who died in April 1941. Upon her husband's death, Rebecca moved to New York where her daughter, Miriam, could be close-by. Miriam's devotion to her mother seemingly superceded a desire to live her own personal life. Miriam had been very close to her father; perhaps she felt an obligation to him to care for her mother. Rebecca Haskell passed away in 1969. But we are getting ahead of our story . . .

Born July 2, 1899, Miriam Haskell was one of the early pioneers for women's rights--a right to exist in the business world. She believed in a woman's privilege of independence. If living a full, independent life, if being a self-made woman due to her keen wit and self-confidence is "eccentric", then this 5'7" slender beauty can be so labeled.

Actually, Miriam Haskell was a young, shrewd, talented businesswoman whose interest in jewelry began when she was proprietor of a gift shop in the exclusive McAlpin Hotel located in New York's then posh Herald Square.

Tales exchanged between collectors of **Miriam Haskell** jewelry have run rampant. One account reports her as a recluse; another states she was an eccentric. Even further out of left field, so to speak, were stories that persisted for years that Miriam Haskell died in poverty, that she lies buried in an unmarked grave, and was a lonesome, homely old maid.

These yarns seem to make Haskell's unique jewelry more "fascinating", and the jewelry produced with her hallmark is more sought-after than some jewelry considered less "notorious". Of course the stories are absurd. **Miriam Haskell** jewelry is truly collectible on its own merit. It's beautifully made, and therefore highly sought as a collectible.

Despite all the baseless rumors, there's every good reason to fancy Miriam Haskell's unique ornamental pieces of jewelry. They were first produced more than a half-century ago in a little shop on

West 57th Street, New York City. Miriam Haskell's innovative jewelry was an **instant** success, so much so, Miss Haskell was able to move her enterprise to "the Avenue" -- Fifth Avenue, New York -- beginning with one upper floor at 392 Fifth Avenue. Her business thrived, and she expanded until the design and manufacture of her ever-popular jewelry took several floors of that building from 1933 until the late sixties.

Her ideas for jewelry were all original, and were copied -- according to Mr. Dubin -- on a regular basis by well-known companies and designers. On a few occasions, so Mr. Dubin reports, "spys were placed in her company to steal designs, particularly during WWII. But they were unmasked. Her competitors were responsible for this, as was discovered on more than one occasion." [The author's Introductory Remarks takes up the matter of "copying" designs, a practice centuries old.]

Miriam Haskell's loyal employees worked many years under her management; some remained to work for subsequent bosses.

It was in the 1920's -- the heart of the Art Deco period -- that Miriam Haskell epitomized what was later to be known in the 1960's as "the jet set". Physically a dark-haired, dark-eyed, fair-skinned beauty, she dressed elegantly and drew around her a choice circle of friends. These she entertained at her ritzy residence on Central Park South, or at her place in the St. Mortiz Hotel, Manhattan. An artisan to the bone, she incorporated all her talents into her jewelry. Her ideas and sketches were produced in complete designs by a young genius, Frank Hess, who designed exclusively for Miriam Haskell. It was a lifelong association which continued even after Miriam sold out her jewelry company to her younger brother, Joseph Haskell, in the early fifties.

Although Frank Hess was her designer, Miriam supervised all production and had the final word of approval. In fact, when Hess was drafted during WWII, the **Miriam Haskell** jewelry business continued to flourish. During those war years, some of Miriam's most original uses of substitute materials were utilized. WWII restrictions on certain metals, and the loss of imported stones from Nazi-conquered countries, forced her adaptation of other media for her fine costume jewelry. It is here that Miriam Haskell's true artistic genius excelled.

Much of the very early **Miriam Haskell** jewelry was unmarked, but **Haskell** jewelry is so unique it is easily recognized once the jewelry is carefully studied. From the late 1930's on, the majority of her pieces have the familiar trademark of an oval escutcheon on the underside of the piece, plainly stamped: **"Miriam Haskell"**. This identification makes it easier for **Haskell** jewelry enthusiasts to collect the pieces which are all still as wearable and enjoyable as when they were first manufactured. The **Miriam Haskell**

mark has remained the same under its three ownerships.

While Miriam Haskell's interest in jewelry continually peaked throughout her long career, she was also involved in other activities. She had several romances, including escorts such as Bernard Gimbel (of department store fame), and Nelson Rockefeller. When she retired, she really did "get out of the business", but her jewelry remained an inspiration to those who followed her lead. Upon retirement, she turned to her avid love of fine art works and her collection of books.

Miriam Haskell did retire due to weariness and illness, but she did not die in poverty; she is not buried in an unmarked grave. To the contrary, she was cared for through her illness by a nephew and his family. She is buried in her beloved city of Louisville, Kentucky. She died July 4, 1981.

Prior to her death, her brother, Joseph Haskell who died June 1977, left a trust fund to care for his sister, Miriam, who was then living in New York. When Mr. Dubin's family received a "distress call" from Aunt Miriam -- "come rescue me . . . bring me to Cinncinati!", they answered the call with open heart and the warmth of a family devoted to her for many years.

Mr. Dubin remembers quite vividly the Ohio River flood disaster of January 1937. He and his mother, (Miriam's "kid sister"), were among the refugees from New Albany, Indiana. While his father remained behind trying to physically salvage what remained of his business, due to water damage, he and his mother were brought to New York City. Miriam Haskell was living at that time in Scarborough-on-the Hudson, (1936-1939). Miriam met the Dubins at the exciting Pennsylvania Station. With her, was an enormous white stuffed sheepdog, as big as 6-year-old nephew, Malcolm. The stuffed animal was named "Manhattan", and Malcom's mother kept it until at age 23, her son joined the U.S. Air Force. From New York City's famous Penn Station, they all travelled via Miriam Haskell's chauffered Packard car, up the scenic Hudson River drive. It had been a sunny winter day, and Dubin's remembrances of that entire event are vivid and recalled most warmly.

Miriam, a soft spoken woman, had a fine vocabularly, was gentle and refined. For two decades, 1930s-1940s, through the depression and even through WWII, Miriam Haskell was known here and abroad as the "First Lady of Fashion".

In the depth of the depression, Miriam Haskell's business was thriving. She was a sharing, concerned person, who thought nothing of giving a doorman a $5 tip, or a waiter $5-$10 tip -- more than most men earned in a day. She was, in the words of her loving nephew, "Miss Generosity!" During WWII, she sent a great deal of money to aid the victims of the "blitz of Britain''. At the height of her earning power, she was exceedingly generous to her family and friends, giving away most of her fortune.

"An elegant figure of a woman,'' says Malcolm Dubin, "who'd stand out in any crowd.''

He might well have been describing **Miriam Haskell** jewelry!

Hobé Cie, Ltd.

[From materials provided by Bruce Hobé, Norman Shapiro, Mildred Combs and Baker Archives]

HOBÉ, ''Jewels of Legendary Splendor'', has a most fascinating background, and a long family history of Parisian born and bred artisan/jewelers.

Jacques Hobé, a master craftsman and foremost maker of jewelry in Paris -- as was his father before him -- had a concept unheard of in his day when only the wealthy owned what we term today as "genuine heirloom'' quality jewelry wrought in gold and precious gems.

It was in 1889 when Jacques Hobé conceived the idea to manufacture fine jewelry at affordable prices, without sacrificing design or quality. He could do this, he decided, by utilizing the efficient manufacturing techniques coming into play during the new "Industrial Revolution'' taking Europe and America by storm.

Design elegance and excellence, he had decided, need not be subordinated by the use of electroplating methods. Thus, he could substitute the more costly gold mountings, while still using handskilled craftsmanship. He could still pay close attention to exquisite details and the hand-setting of ornamental gemstones in place of the more expensive precious gems.

When Jacques Hobé's son, William, brought his own jeweler's art to America, he carried on the admired tradition of his father, earning for himself a following of famed Hollywood stars and producers, due to his unique jewelry and costume designs. The jewelry complemented his costume designs.

Hobé process in electrolytic plating is exclusive -- "FORMULA 70'' -- which uses a 22 karat electrolytic gold guaranteed by a five year warranty. It was William Hobé who located the firm in New York, where his designer sons, Donald and Robert, carry on his work.

Bruce Hobé, grandson of its founder, is **Hobé's** Western Sales Manager.

In 1964, **Hobé** created heirloom replicas from original jewels worn in the French, Spanish and Austrian Courts. Made of gold-toned metal embellished with multi-colored enamels, many of the pieces were hand-set with cultured pearls and real ornamental gemstones such as turquoise, lapis, malachite, tiger eye, agate and jade. These "soft-stone'' ornamental stones and beads were set to enhance the beautiful mountings. The **Hobé** brothers are experts in fine jade, and are selective in their use of both genuine and imitation paste stones. The replica heirloom pieces included pendants, rings, bracelets and earrings. A highlight of this showing was a magnificient replica of "The Croix de Richelieu'', featured in the exclusive collection at Robinson's, (Beverly Hills, California).

Exclusive reproductions of antique jewelry executed in hand-enamelled mountings set with garnets and turquoise were featured in Saks Fifth Avenue stores in Beverly Hills and Palm Springs, California.

Marshall Field & Company, offered **Hobé** jewelry "influenced by the Orient with a look of hammered gold''. This uniquely designed jewelry, made of thin gold-colored metal "wafers'', were etched and *pavé*-set with tiny square-cut rhinestones.

The Chicago-based firm, C.D. Peacock Jewelers, (established in 1837), had an exclusive showing of "Courtly Splendor'' by **Hobé**. These high fashion costume jewelry pieces were individual works of artisanship, largely handmade and advertised as "gold filled filigree on sterling silver with well cut, multi-colored imitation stones and some semi-precious stones, cameos and hand-painted miniatures on ivory''. The important feature was the fact that there were no two pieces exactly alike. Even though advertised as "Costume Jewelry'', the earrings alone commanded $39--a goodly sum in the early 1960's. Today, those collectible high fashion **Hobé** jewelry pieces, bring better than triple the price or more.

Hobé has an exclusive multi-million dollar contract with the largest pearl manufacturing plant in Majorca. The Island of Majorca (Spain), is famous for its internationally acclaimed man-made pearls which so closely duplicate the luminous beauty of cultured pearls. (See PEARLS in Glossary).

Hobé is one of the most highly respected and sought after names in the collectible field of high fashion costume jewelry. For those familiar with **Hobé** jewelry, past and present, this is entirely understandable.

Hobé's national showrooms are located in New York, Los Angeles, Dallas and Denver.

Kenneth Jay Lane, Inc.

[Courtesy of Genevieve M. Dawson, Publicity,
Kenneth Jay Lane, Inc.; *K.J. Lane; Baker archives]*

In New York's posh Trump Tower, there's a popular fashion facility known as **Kenneth Jay Lane Shop.** London and Paris based shops call K.J.L. shops, simply **Ken Lane Shops.** Anyone, since the mid-sixties, who has been a high fashion jewelry buff, knows all too well who "Ken Lane" is.

Ken was born in Detroit, Michigan, where he attended the University of Michigan, followed by enrollment at the Rhode Island School of Design. There he earned a degree in Advertising Design.

His sights were on establishing a reputation in "the big city" -- New York -- where he was first employed as part of the promotion staff of *Vogue* magazine. Through his very first job at *Vogue*, he was fortunate to meet and befriend Roger Vivier, famed designer. Through Vivier, Kenneth Jay Lane became assistant designer for "Delman Shoes". Shortly thereafter, Ken's talents were recognized and appreciated by "Christian Dior Shoes" where he became associate designer for this famous name in the fashion field. Too, this job enabled him to spend part of each year working in Paris with Vivier, who no doubt appreciated Ken's talent and nurtured it.

In 1963, while still designing shoes, Ken began making a few pieces of unique jewelry from his own designs. These were primarily earrings. Several of these ear-drop eye-catchers were photographed by top fashion magazines, and soon orders began to arrive from a few fine shops. Ken was literally "on his way", when all his ingenious pieces were sold out on the first day of sale at Saks Fifth Avenue -- an exclusive advertising event for **"Kenneth Jay Lane Jewelry".**

While Ken continued designing shoes during his daytime job, he made his jewelry at night and on weekends. Within a year, "K.J.L." jewelry was selling "big" in such stores as Neiman-Marcus, Bonwit Teller, Henri Bendel and Saks Fifth Avenue across the country. Re-orders were coming in fast and furious, until his part-time jewelry business became his full-time career. His creative ambitions were recognized and realized.

A highlight in Ken's life came in 1966, when he was recipient of the **Coty American Fashion Critic's Special Award,** for "outstanding contribution to fashion through one of the correlative fields". Hard on the heels of this prestigious award, came recognition from Neiman-Marcus, Harper's Bazaar, Tobé Coburn and many other outstanding industry awards and citations.

The designer/manufacturer, Kenneth Jay Lane, is a trend-setting, witty and colorful character whose high fashion costume jewelry has captured the scene of many "social seasons". His "fabulous fakery", contrived with use of cabachon shapes of colored plastics, mounted in oddly shaped metals giving additional charm and ingenuity to his work, are much in demand and daringly worn.

Among his famous customers who have been charmed, are members of the royal families abroad, oil-barons' wives, New York's "Blue Book" of high society and a full worldwide clientele from New York to Australia and the Continent.

Although a millionaire now in his own right, Kenneth Jay Lane began very modestly with a staff of two -- himself and a girl Friday. That was in 1963. To date, as President of **Kenneth Jay Lane, Inc.,** Ken's business has flourished into a large profit-sharing organization. But no matter how big the business has grown, he has never lost a sense of humility so admirable in one so successful.

In response to a question about his success and advice about how to achieve it under the American free enterprise system, Ken maintains that the opportunity is here for those willing to work long hours to achieve ones goal. Of course, he admits that a little talent and some imagination helps. If one has those, and the ability to discipline oneself and utilize the hours in a day, Ken insists "there are still plenty of opportunities around."

Ken describes himself as one who has "a little talent" -- a modest remark. It belies the record of huge demands for his original jewelry conceptions, his bold uses of imitation gems and mountings. All this holds much appeal to wearers and collectors of **K.J.L.** jewelry of all kinds. His jewelry is not just for today, but enjoys a heyday with high fashion jewelry collectors of his earlier pieces.

Kenneth Jay Lane's use of innovative plastic stones have been accepted, approved, favored and sought out; his jewelry has been continually in demand for more than two decades. Already, **K.J.L.** jewelry is a staple in any worthwhile and representative collection of high fashion jewelry.

Section II

Color Plates & Descriptions

Black & White Photographs & Descriptions

Illustrations & Descriptions

Drawings & Advertisements

Plate 1

Location	Nomenclature	Circa	Description
Top, Left	BROOCH	1945	**Hobé.** Ivory Chessman, 3¾" x 2½" mounted in gold-tone, w/faceted bezel set amethyst, tourmaline, peridot and other gemstones.
Top, Right	EARRINGS	1945	**Hobé.** Bezel set blue zircons, amethyst, peridot and topaz gemstones. Gold-tone 1" x 1½" mounting. Adjustable screw-back earrings.
Middle	NECKLACE	1960	**Boucher.** Flexible florentine finish gold-tone w/*faux* Persian turquoise and prong-set rhinestones.
Center, Top	BROOCH	1960	**Boucher.** Brushed antique finish, w/rhinestones.
Center, Bottom	PIN	1960	**Boucher.** "March Hare", marked with "B" on tail & **Pat. design #9089.** Red glass eye and black enamel nose. *(Barbara L. Hammell Collection)*

Plate 1.
Dr. N.J. Williams Collection unless otherwise noted.

Plate 2

Location	Nomenclature	Circa	Description
Top	PIN	1960	**Emmons.** "Crown Jewel", with *faux* cabachons and rhinestones in patented goldtone.
Row 2	Set: PIN & EARRINGS	1950	**Emmons.** Topaz color glass set in goldtone. Clip earrings.
Center	Set: PENDANT & EARRINGS	1960	**Emmons.** Cabachon glass and cultured pearls set in patented goldtone. Detachable tassels. Clip earrings.
Bottom	Set: BROOCH & EARRINGS	1960	**Emmons.** *Faux* moonstones and imitation gemstones.

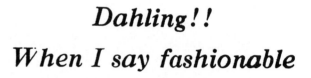

Dahling!!
When I say fashionable

I mean—

EMMONS JEWELRY

Credit: Eleanor Musser Archives

Plate 2.
Elaine Dill collection.

Plate 3

Location	Nomenclature	Circa	Description
Left	BRACELET	1930	**Unmarked.** Art Deco linked Bakelite.
Right	PENDANT	1925	**Unmarked.** Brass and Bakelite. King Tut Tomb opening influenced this trend in fashion jewelry. Plastic beads and brass spacers. Art Deco period.
Center, Left	PENDANT	1925	**Unmarked.** Brass ornament mounted on Bakelite w/enamelling. Art Deco, King Tut, Egyptian influence.
Center, Right	BROOCH	1930	**Jeanne.** Brass and plastic. Art Deco.
Center	BROOCH	1935	**Unmarked.** Carved amber resin with molded and hand detailed black plastic cameo.
Bottom, Center	BROOCH	1935	**Unmarked.** Carved amber resin, Art Deco wing design, accented by a carved black plastic scarab. Egyptian influence.
Bottom	BRACELETS	1935	**Unmarked.** Bakelite bangles in mottled plastic.

Plate 3.
Author's collection.

Plate 4

Location	Nomenclature	Circa	Description
Left	CROSS, w/adjustable 24″ chain	1970	**Emmons.** "Royalty". Set with plastic turquoise and cultured pearl. Painted enamel. Rhodium mounting.
Top, Center	Set: PIN & EARRINGS	1970	**Emmons.** "Blue Bud". Faceted glass in burnished rhodium.
Center	Set: BROOCH & EARRINGS	1960	**Emmons.** Painted enamel on rhodium with *faux* turquoise stones.
Center, Bottom	Each: AWARD PIN & MEDALLION	1965-66	**Emmons.** Recruiting award and medallion commemorating new **Emmons'** facility.
Top, Right	BRACELET	1950	**Emmons.** Plastic in rhodium. (Available in pink or white with necklace and earrings.)
Bottom, Right	CROSS	1977	**Emmons.** "Regency". Antiqued rhodium, filigree, with applied beading. (Chain available)

Plate 4.
Elaine Dill collection.

Plate 5 Location	Nomenclature	Circa	Description
Top	EARRINGS	1960	**Emmons.** Simulated pearls set in rhodium. Matching necklace not shown. Clip earrings.
Center & Bottom	*PARURE:* Necklace, Earrings & Bracelet	1967	**"Celebration: Queen Elizabeth"**, by **Emmons.** Rhodium and rhinestone replica of coronation jewels. (This was a gift for Hostess of an **Emmons** Jewelry Fashion Show.)

EMMONS Jewelry

Magic Lantern's Compatibility

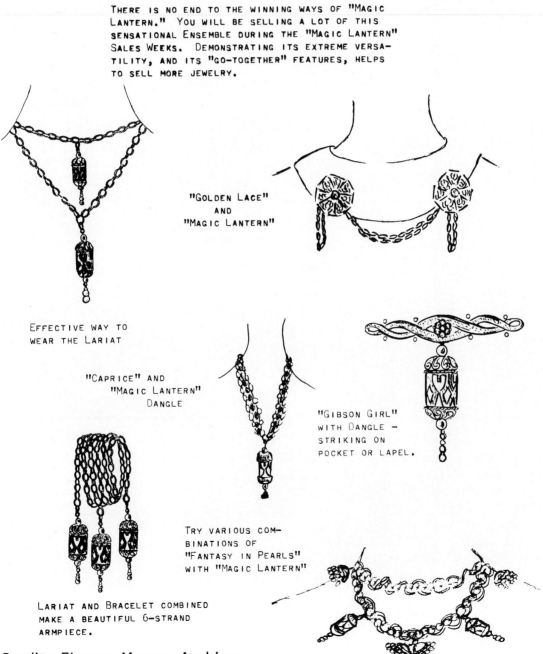

THERE IS NO END TO THE WINNING WAYS OF "MAGIC LANTERN." YOU WILL BE SELLING A LOT OF THIS SENSATIONAL ENSEMBLE DURING THE "MAGIC LANTERN" SALES WEEKS. DEMONSTRATING ITS EXTREME VERSATILITY, AND ITS "GO-TOGETHER" FEATURES, HELPS TO SELL MORE JEWELRY.

"GOLDEN LACE" AND "MAGIC LANTERN"

EFFECTIVE WAY TO WEAR THE LARIAT

"CAPRICE" AND "MAGIC LANTERN" DANGLE

"GIBSON GIRL" WITH DANGLE – STRIKING ON POCKET OR LAPEL.

TRY VARIOUS COMBINATIONS OF "FANTASY IN PEARLS" WITH "MAGIC LANTERN"

LARIAT AND BRACELET COMBINED MAKE A BEAUTIFUL 6-STRAND ARMPIECE.

Credit: Eleanor Musser Archives

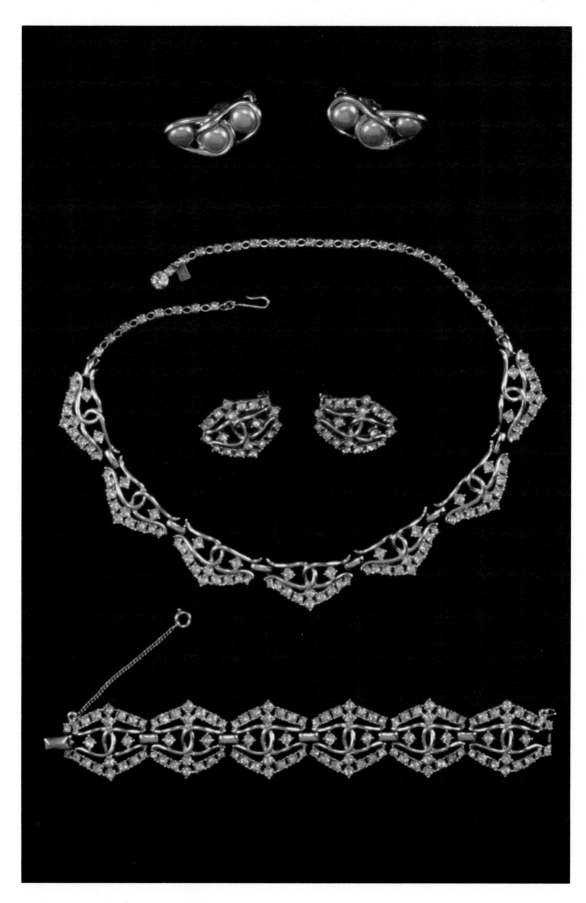

Plate 5.
Ethel Wilson collection.

Plate 6

Location	Nomenclature	Circa	Description
Row 1, L - R	Set: PIN & EARRINGS	1960	**Emmons.** Simulated pearls and rhinestones set in goldtone. Clip earrings. Emmons was the first to introduce ½ pair (or a third earring), in case of loss.
Row 2, L - R	Set: PIN & EARRINGS	1960	**Emmons.** Etched and engraved burnished goldtone, set with simulated pearls and rhinestones. Clip earrings.
Row 3, L - R	Set: PIN & EARRINGS	1960	**Emmons.** Simulated pearls and *faux* gemstones in goldtone.
Bottom, Left	PIN	1950	**Emmons.** "Dearest" pin. Simulated gemstones spell word. Diamond, Emerald, Amethyst, Ruby, Emerald, Sapphire, Topaz. *Faux* pearls. Patented goldtone. Victorian love-brooch influence.
Bottom, Right	PIN	1954	**Emmons.** "**Bobcat**". Limited edition souvenir given to **Emmons** Jewelry Fashion Show Directors during a special Bob Crosby's TV "**Bobcat Show**". Antiqued goldtone figural with green eye accent. *Author's collection.*

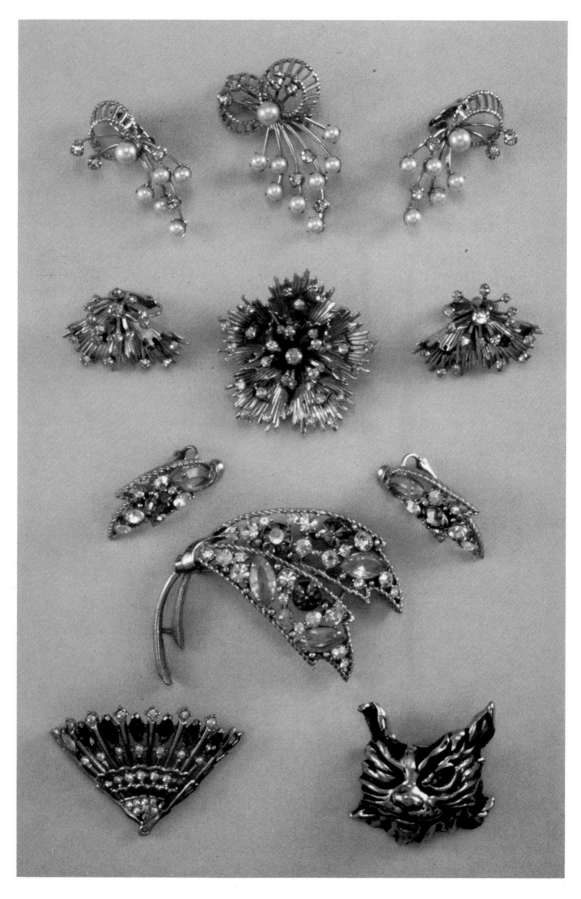

Plate 6.
Ethel Wilson collection unless otherwise noted.

Plate 7

Location	Nomenclature	Circa	Description
Top	PIN	1948	**Hobe′**, tri-colored genuine gemstones, bezel set in filigree gold-tone. Large 2¾″ x 1½″ pin.
Row 2, L - R	Set: RING & EARRINGS	1948	**Hobe′**, antiqued gold-tone, screw-back earrings. Both pieces are set with genuine moonstones, amethysts and various genuine gemstones.
Center	BOW PIN w/LOCKET	1948	**Hobe′**, detachable heart-shaped locket. *Vermicelli* work, bezel set moonstones. Pastel color genuine gemstones set in antiqued gold-tone.
Row 3	EARRINGS	1948	**Hobe′**. Dainty screw-back earrings, 1¼″ x 1″, with multi-color genuine gemstones.
Row 4	CAMEO BROOCH	1948	**Hobe′**. Exquisite shell cameo brooch, with pear-cut drops. Bezel set genuine gemstones.
Bottom	EARRINGS	1948	**Hobe′**, 1¾″ x 1″ leaf design clip earrings. Faceted and bezel set genuine gemstones. Antiqued gold-tone.

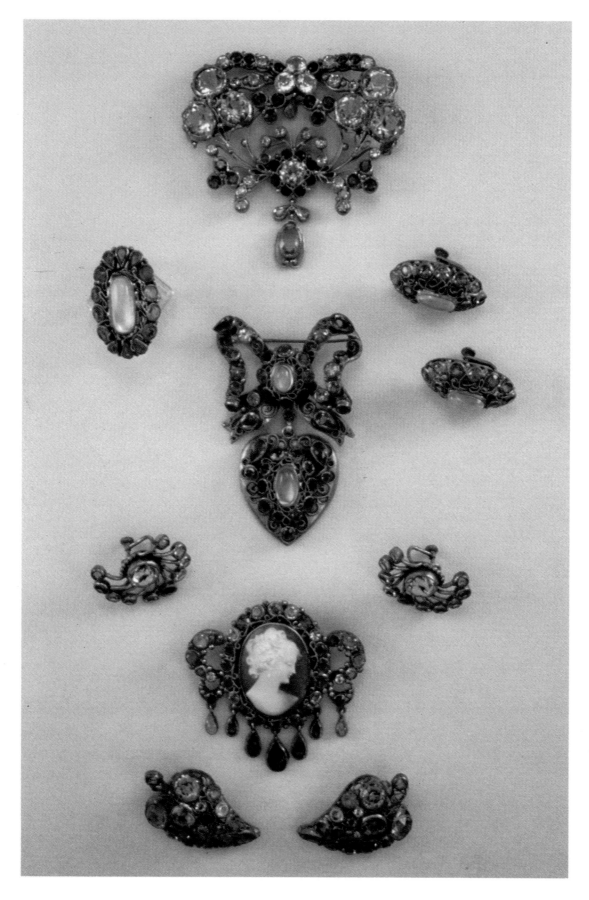

Plate 7.
Dr. N.J. Williams collection.

Plate 8

Location	Nomenclature	Circa	Description
Left	CHAIN	1960	**Sarah Coventry.** Rhodium. Sold as an accessory to 3/piece set shown on this Plate.
Center & Top Right	*PARURE:* Bracelet, Earrings, & Brooch	1960	**Sarah Coventry.** **"Celebrity"** edition. *Parure* in rhodium set with smoky color faceted glass and prong-set rhinestones.
Bottom, Right	Set: PIN & EARRINGS	1960	**Sarah Coventry.** **"Snowflake"**, rhodium set with smoky color faceted glass accented with rhinestones.

Plate 8.
Mary Harrington collection.

Plate 9

Location	Nomenclature	Circa	Description
Top Row, L - R	PIN	1962	**Ledo.** *Pave'* set, pear shaped and baquette cut *faux* gemstones in goldtone.
	PIN	1955-65	**Trifari.** Basket design, set with baquette and pear shaped topaz color stones and clear rhinestones.
	PIN	1960	**Trifari.** *Pave'.* set rhinestones. Art Moderne stylized bird.
Row 2, L - R	PIN	1960	**Trifari.** Enamelled figural dragonfly.
	PIN	1960	**Trifari.** Beautifully enamelled floral with rhinestone accents on stamen and leaves.
	PIN	1960	**Trifari.** Tiny goldtone "scatter" pin.
Row 3, L - R	PIN	1965	**Trifari.** Gold electroplate, enamel, set with cultured pearls.
	PIN	1965	**Trifari.** Goldtone figural dog "scatter" pin.
	PIN	1955	**Trifari.** Enamel on gold electroplate. (Popularized again in 1985)
Bottom	PIN	1960	**Trifari.** Goldtone feather design scarf pin.

Plate 9.
Allison Dickason collection.

Plate 10

Location	Nomenclature	Circa	Description
Left & Top	Set: EARRINGS & BRACELET	1950	**Sarah Coventry.** Art Moderne design in rhodium.
Center & Right Top to Bottom	*PARURE:* Bracelet, Earrings, & Brooch	1960	**Sarah Coventry, "Vienna"** design. Bohemian black "jet" glass, possibly from Jablonecer, (Czech. area). Faceted rhinestines set in rhodium. Trademark appears on the clasp. Earrings are marked on each clip: "right" & "left" ear.

Plate 10.
Mary Harrington collection.

Plate 11

Location	Nomenclature	Circa	Description
Top Row	Set: BROOCH W/dangle or button-type clip EARRINGS	1970	**Emmons.** Filigree mounted imitation glass gemstones. Patented goldtone. Pendant earrings are convertible to wire for pierced ears.
Center	Set: BROOCH & EARRINGS	1960	**Emmons.** Antiqued goldtone with aurora borealis stones. Clip earrings.
Bottom, L - R	PIN	1960	**Emmons, "Lambkin".** Oxidized brass and painted enamel.
	PIN	1960	**Emmons.** Painted enamel on goldtone, set with simulated pearls, coral and turquoise. (Earrings available).
	PIN	1960	**Emmons.** Painted enamel on goldtone. Although of the Art Moderne period, this design has Art Deco influence.

Plate 11.
Elaine Dill collection.

Plate 12

Location	Nomenclature	Circa	Description
Top	PIN	1960	**Castlecliff.** Gold electroplate with simulated baroque pearl. *Allison Dickason collection.*
Center	NECKLACE	1960	**Original by Robért.** Gilded bead separators with cupped simulated pearls, in baroque and seed shapes. (Note similarity between **Robért** and **Haskell jewelry**.) *Allison Dickason collection.*
Center	BROOCH	1950	**Miriam Haskell.** Faceted, unfoiled Austrian crystal, combined with numerous crystal beads and rhinestones, clustered on a gold electroplated mounting. Unique design. *Allison Dickason collection.*
Bottom, Left	Set: PIN & EARRINGS	1950	**Boucher.** Bamboo design, with enamelling. Gold electroplate. Clip earrings. *Mildred Combs collection.*
Bottom, Right	PIN	1950	**Boucher.** Scarf pin. Goldtone and enamelled. *Mildred Combs collection.*

Plate 12.

Plate 13

Location	Nomenclature	Circa	Description
Row 1, L - R	EARRINGS	1967	Marked: "**Chr. Dior**" (Christian Dior), and "**Germany**". *Faux* jade & sapphires. Clip earrings.
	PIN	1967	**Christian Dior.** Cabachon German glass *faux* lapis and turquoise.
	EARRINGS	1940	**Miriam Haskell.** Wired turquoise and blue glass stones, combined with gilded filigree mounting.
Row 2, Left	FUR CLIP	1950	**Mazer.** Unfoiled Bohemian red glass, and varied cut rhinestones, set in rhodium and goldtone.
Row 2, Right	PIN	1960	**Coro.** Crown design, set wtih cabachon style *faux* stones and rhinestones. Goldtone mounting. *Author's collection.*
Row 3, Center	PIN	1950	**Vendome.** Prong-set multi-cut stones. Antiqued copper lustre, with japanned center mount.
Row 4	BEADS	1960	**Unmarked.** Four-strand Austrian aurora borealis beads. *Sybel Heller collection.*

Plate 13.
G.L. Antiques collection, unless otherwise noted.

Plate 14

Location	Nomenclature	Circa	Description
Top, Left	BROOCH	1960	**Sarah Covenry.** Marked: "S.C.", this is a limited edition **Lady Coventry** collection, sold in a lovely velvet and satin box. Jade and cultured pearls in goldtone.
Bottom, Left	BROOCH	1950	**Sarah Coventry,** "Seeds of Wheat" design. Goldtone, with granular work. This brooch complements bracelet shown on this Plate.
Center	BRACELET	1950	**Sarah Coventry.** "Harvest Wheat" design. Antique goldtone.
Top, Right	HAIR BARRETT	1950	**Sarah Coventry.** Florentine goldtone, set with a cultured small pearl. Hair barretts are once again popular since the 1970's.
Bottom, Right	PIN	1950	**Sarah Coventry.** Stylized flower set with rhinestones and pronged amber glass. Patented goldtone.

Plate 14.
Mary Harrington collection.

Plate 15

Location	Nomenclature	Circa	Description
Top	BROOCH	1960	**Mimi.** Ribbon design, with prong-set and faceted rhinestones.
Center	BRACELET	1960	**Weiss.** Flexible links, in rhodium. Prong-set Austrian rhinestones.
Bottom	Set: EARRINGS & NECKLACE	1950	**Napier.** Antiqued and oxidized metallic mountings for exquisitely cut and faceted rhinestones. Large brilliant drops.

Plate 15.
Janet St.Amant collection.

Plate 16

Location	Nomenclature	Circa	Description
Top Row	EARRINGS	1960	**Nettie Rosenstein.** Gold electroplate with *pave'* set rhinestones. Clip earrings.
Row 2, L - R	PIN	1960	**Boucher.** Marked: "Pat.Pend. 3453". Cultured pearl and rhinestones. Gold electroplate.
	PIN	1967	**Christian Dior.** 24K gold electroplate, set with rhinestones. Marked: "**Chr. Dior** ©**1967 Germany**".
	PIN	1940	**Mazer.** Sterling with gold wash, *(vermeil)*. Cultured pearl and finely cut rhinestones. Back is marked: "B".
Row 3	BRACELET	1950	**Nettie Rosenstein.** Fabulous *pave'* set rhinestones in goldtone.
Row 4 & 5	*PARURE:* Necklace, Earrings & Bracelet	1960	**Trifari.** Cast electroplated mounting with fine faceted rhinestones. *Sybel Heller collection.*

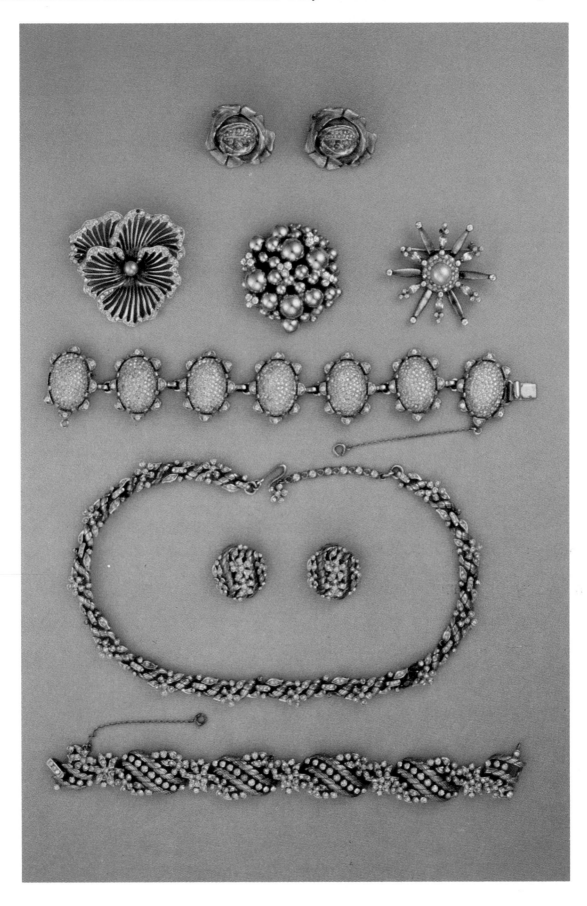

Plate 16.
G.L. Antiques collection, unless otherwise noted.

Plate 17

Location	Nomenclature	Circa	Description
Top, Left	PIN	1950	**Coro.** Figural peacock. Enamel on gold electroplate.
Bottom, Left	PIN	1955	**Marvella.** Simulated jade and engraved spokes on fan. Gold electroplate.
Top Center	BROOCH	1950	**Swoboda.** Gold electroplate, cast mold to simulate granular work. Carved jade and cultured pearls.
Center & Right	Set: PENDANT & EARRINGS	1950	**HAR.** Etched and engraved goldtone, set with imitation glass. Hand cast and molded with applied beading. (Replica of an antique design).
Top, Right	EARRINGS	1960	**Vendome.** Gold electroplated earrings. Enamel. Adjustable screw-back clip. *Allison Dickason collection.*
Bottom, Right	EARRINGS	1960	**Mosell.** Popular shell design. Handpainted gold electroplated clip earrings.

Plate 17.
Mildred Combs collection, unless otherwise noted.

Plate 18

Location	Nomenclature	Circa	Description
Top Row, Left	PIN	1950	**Emmons.** "**Rainbow Star**" design. Aurora borealis stones and cultured pearl in goldtone.
Top Row, Right	RING	1970	**Emmons.** Aurora borealis *pave'* set stones in goldtone.
Center & Bottom	*PARURE:* Earrings, Necklace & Bracelet	1970	**Emmons.** "**First Lady**" design. Presented to America's First Lady, Pat Nixon. Cultured pearls in rhodium.

Plate 18.
Ethel Wilson collection.

Plate 19

Location	Nomenclature	Circa	Description
Top, L - R	Set: BROOCH w/EARRINGS	1948	**Hobe'.** 2¾″ x 1¾″ heart-shaped antiqued gold-tone pin with tri-color genuine gemstones, including a large citrine. Clip earrings: 1¼″ x ⅞″. All gemstones are bezel set.
Center	PIN	1945	**Josef.** 4½″ extended bar. Oxidized brass, with tassel.
Bottom	"DOG COLLAR" NECKLACE	1950	**Monet.** 15½″ chain with adjustable slide and tassles. Slide is engraved: **"N.J.W."** Variations of "The Gibson Adjustable Collar", appeared in Monet Master Jeweler advertisements in leading fashion magazines. April 1950, *Flair*, (out-of-print), showed a full page ad reading: "Monet's new 'dog collar' with the adjustable slide to fit your neck perfectly . . . In the Golden Manner of Monet." The necklace came with matching earrings and bracelet, all sold separately. Each piece had the **Monet** signature.

The Fashion Academy, which selects America's ten best-dressed women, awarded its first gold medal in the jewelry field to **Monet**, and this fine jewelry company proudly announced this recognition with their slogan: **FASHION ACADEMY AWARD WINNER FOR FASHION LEADERSHIP IN JEWELRY**. Notice the absence of any reference to "costume jewelry". At long last, high fashion jewelry had come of age.

Plate 19.
Dr. N.J. Williams and Barbara L. Hammell collection.

Plate 20

Location	Nomenclature	Circa	Description
Full Plate	Set: EARRINGS & NECKLACE	1950	**Napier.** Gold electroplated signets and hearts on waist-length chain. Can be worn as a decorative belt.

Plate 20.
Janet St. Amant collection.

Plate 21

Location	Nomenclature	Circa	Description
Row 1, Left	EARRINGS	1945	**Hattie Carnegie.** *Pave'* set rhinestones in rhodium. Art Moderne design. *Mary Ruth Evry Collection.*
Row 1, Right	DRESS CLIP	1930-40	**Eisenberg.** (box not shown). Sterling w/gold wash, *(vermeil),* with large magnificently faceted and cut rhinestones. *Estelle Keevil Tyson collection.*
Row 2	EARRINGS	1970	**K.J.L. (Kenneth Jay Lane).** Antiqued metal with *faux* smoky topaz and citrines. Exceptionally large pendants. *Mary Ruth Evry collection.*
Row 3	BRACELET	1950	**Eisenberg.** Variety of cut and faceted fine rhinestones set in rhodium. *Mary Ruth Evry collection*
Bottom, Left	EARRINGS	1950	**Eisenberg.** Rhinestone and rhodium drops. *Mary Ruth Evry collection.*
Bottom, Right	EARRINGS	1940	**Jomaz.** Blue glass cabachons and rhinestones. Clip type earrings. *Estelle Keevil Tyson collection.*

Plate 21.

Plate 22

Location	Nomenclature	Circa	Description
Top Row	BRACELET	1950	**Eisenberg.** Rhodium and rhinestones.
Row 2	BRACELET	1940	**Eisenberg Ice.** Special patented clasp. Rhodium and rhinestones.
Row 3	Set: BROOCH & EARRINGS	1940	**Eisenberg Ice.** Exceptionally large brooch with multi-cut rhinestones set in rhodium. Clip earrings.
Row 4	NECKLACE	1950	**Weiss.** Exquisitely designed necklace, hand-cut and set, faceted rhinestones in rhodium.
Row 4, Center	Set: EARRINGS & PIN	1950	**Eisenberg.** Rhinestones in rhodium. Clip earrings.
Bottom	BRACELET	1960	**Eisenberg.** Individually linked, flexible bracelet of rhodium, set with rhinestones.

E I S E N B E R G   I C E [Eisenberg Designs Copyrighted]

the year of the ear...

As seen in HARPER'S BAZAAR

[March 1967 advertisement]

[Karl Eisenberg Archives]   [Drawings from ad by W.C.Baker]

Plate 22.
Allison Dickason collection.

Plate 23

Location	Nomenclature	Circa	Description
Top	Set: EARRINGS & NECKLACE	1960	**Mazer.** Gold electroplated mounting set with rhinestones and *faux* topaz stone. Art Moderne influence. *Author's collection.*
Row 2, Left	BROOCH	1950	**DeNicola, "St. George Killing the Dragon"**, novelty brooch. Antiqued goldtone, with *pave'* set rhinestones and *faux* gemstones. *June Forest collection.*
Row 2, Right	BROOCH	1950	**CoroCraft.** Novelty brooch, marked: "sterling", with gold wash *(vermeil)*. Set with *faux* Persian turquoise and rhinestones. Depicts a band on stage. Expert workmanship and detail. *June Forest collection.*
Bottom	*PARURE:* Earrings, Necklace & Bracelet	1960	**Weiss.** Unusual yellow opaque glass stones with crystal beads. Clip earrings. *Peggy Covey collection, owner of the Aamber Jelly Bean, Los Angeles.*

Plate 23.

Plate 24

Location	Nomenclature	Circa	Description
Top, Left	PIN	1960	**Van Dell.** Simulated moonstones and blue *faux* gemstones. Mounting marked: "⅟₂₀ 12K GEP" = ⅟₂₀th of 12Karat Gold Electroplate. Pin has a small loop to accomodate a chain. *Mildred Combs collection.*
Top, Right	PIN	1960	**Symmetalic.** *Vermeil*, (14K over sterling). Simulated moonstones. *Mildred Combs collection.*
Center	BEADS	1960	**DeMario.** Necklace of multi-color blue beads strung on chain. Probably Czechoslavakian beads. *Mildred Combs collection.*
Center	PIN	1950	**Weiss.** Multi-color faceted Bohemian glass in oxidized gilded brass mounting. *Author's collection.*
Bottom, Left	PIN	1960	**Coro.** *Vermeil*, (gold wash over sterling) set with simulated stones. *Mildred Combs collection.*
Bottom, Right	PIN	1955	**Boucher.** Painted enamel figural fish. *Allison Dickason collection.*

Plate 24.

Plate 25

Location	Nomenclature	Circa	Description
Top, Right	PIN	1960	**Kramer.** Butterfly design. Multi-color blue sets in goldtone. *Lynn Warech collection.*
Center	BROOCH	1960	**Unmarked.** Exceptionally large brooch set with unfoiled Austrian aurora borealis stones and rhinestones, all prong-set in gold electroplated mounting. *G.L. Antiques collection.*
Top Left, Center & Bottom	*PARURE:* Earrings, Bracelet & Necklace	1950	**Unmarked.** Bohemian finely cut and faceted aurora borealis stones, prong-set in rhodium mounting. Fabulous collar design. Clip earrings and flexible bracelet. *Lynn Warech collection.*

Plate 25.

Plate 26

Location	Nomenclature	Circa	Description
Top	PIN	1950	**Weiss.** Gold electroplated heart-shaped mounting set with *faux* rubies.
Top Left	FUR CLIP	1930	**Eisenberg.** Unique pink and crystal rhinestones. Very large and heavy metallic mounting, gold electroplated.
Top, Right	EARRINGS	1935	**Schaiparelli.** Pink rhinestones and *faux* prong-set pearl with large rhinestone center.
Center	BROOCH	1935-40	**Nettie Rosenstein.** Sterling, set with rose quartz and genuine jade.
Bottom, Center, L - R	Set: BROOCH & EARRINGS	1940	**Nettie Rosenstein.** Floral motif, with green onyx and rhinestones.
Bottom, Left	EARRINGS (Clip)	1960	**Mosell.** Popular shell design. Handpainted. Gold electroplate; cast mold. (See Plate 17 for another shell design).
Bottom, Right	FUR CLIP	1930	**Trifari.** Double-pronged. Fuschia, enamelled and *pave'* set with rhinestones. *Author's collection.*

Plate 26.
Estelle Keevil Tyson collection, unless otherwise noted.

Plate 27A (Opposite)

Location	Nomenclature	Circa	Description
Top to Bottom	NECKLACE	1955-65	**Yves. St. Laurent.** Extraordinary hammered and etched antiqued German silver. Innovative clasp. Design may have been inspired by George Braque's **"Birds in Flight"**. (See Plate 27B below). *Allison Dickason collection.*

Plate 27B (Below)

Original etching, **"Birds In Flight"**, by George Braque. *Author's collection.*

Plate 27B.

Plate 27A.

Plate 28

Location	Nomenclature	Circa	Description
Top, Left	PIN	1942	**"Golden Clover"** remembrance pin. An original design exclusive with **Tyrrell Jewelers, Inc.**, Oakland, California. Each of the four sections of the clover signifies the four words: **To - Mother - With - Love**. The pin is 14K gold with a certified and registered diamond. The advertising booklet reads: "Far from home and often homesick, your son thinks of you. But since tender words do not come easily to a young man, he has chosen this pure gold and diamond pin to speak for him. It was designed by a young serviceman who, like your own boy, found this way to say . . . *'Mother, I love you'* We hope it will bring you happiness and good luck. *Wear this lucky Clover of Gold With its diamond pure and true And let the heart-shaped petals speak Your son's devotion to you."* *Author's collection.*
Top, Right	EARRINGS	1950	**Trifari.** Classic style rhodium clip earrings. *Author's collection.*
Center, Top	BROOCH	1950	**Schreiner, N.Y.** - Bezel set cabachons of amber color glass. *Author's collection.*
Bottom, Center	PENDANT	1965	**Trifari.** Large, amber color bezel set impressive cabachon, with gold electroplated wire "choke collar". *Dr. N.J. Williams collection.*
Bottom	CHAIN	1965	**Trifari.** A four-strand goldtone chain necklace. **"Trifari"** on small tag. *Sybel Heller collection.*

Plate 28.

Plate 29

Location	Nomenclature	Circa	Description
Top, Left	PIN	1960	**Boucher.** Blackamoor, painted enamel on goldtone with *faux* gemstones.
Top, Right	SCARF PIN	1955-65	**Trifari.** Sterling *vermeil*, (gilded silver) with *faux* gemstones. *Mildred Combs collection.*
Row 2, L - R	EARRINGS	1960	**Trifari.** Cabachons prong-set in goldtone with *pave'* set rhinestones.
	EARRINGS	1960	**Hattie Carnegie.** Cabachons, bezel set *faux* sapphires, in goldtone.
	EARRINGS	1955-60	**Miriam Haskell.** Unique design, with prong-set imitation stones.
Row 3, L - R	PIN	1960	**HAR.** Goldtone figural, with imitation stone accents. Cast mounting.
	EARRINGS	1970	**KJL (Kenneth Jay Lane).** *Faux* coral and emerald with seed pearls.
	PIN	1960	**HAR.** Goldtone figural with imitation stone accents. Cast mounting.
Row 4, L - R	SCARF PIN	1955-65	**Accessocraft.** Gold electroplate.
	FUR CLIP	1930	**Eisenberg Original.** Gilded silver with *faux* gemstones.
	PIN	1940	**Trifari.** Sterling *vermeil* figural. Cast mounting with uniquely cut Bohemian crystal. Rhinestone accents.

Plate 29.
Allison Dickason collection unless otherwise noted.

Plate 30

Location	Nomenclature	Circa	Description
Top Row	EARRINGS	1960	**Eisenberg Ice.** Clip earrings with blue and pink imitation zircons. *Allison Dickason collection.*
Row 2, Left	BROOCH	1947	**Cini.** Etched and engraved sterling. Original "**Capicorn**" design by Guglielmo Cini. This is one of the Zodiac series, **Cini's** 1947 contribution to fashionable jewelry, celebrative of **Cini's** 25th anniversary as an American jewelry designer and craftsman. Zodiac designs were also made in 14K gold, in the exact same design as in sterling. *Jenny Biddle collection.*
Row 2, Center	BROOCH	1940	**Cini.** Handwrought in sterling. Pair of cupids playing lyre. **Cini** created sterling handwrought jewelry since 1922. *Author's collection.*
Row 2, Right	BROOCH	1940	**Cini.** Handwrought sterling. Baroque floral design, always a popular motif. Guglielmo Cini arrived in America at age 17. He was already an accomplished creator of fine jewelry. Once established in the United States, his patrons included stars of stage and screen. For many years, his studio was located in Laguna Beach, California. *Jenny Biddle collection.*
Row 3	BRACELET	1950	**Cini.** Cast in sterling, then hand-finished. *Jenny Biddle collection.*
Row 4, Left	BROOCH	1950	**Weiss.** Very large figural butterfly. Japanned mounting with uniquely cut and faceted rhinestones. *Mildred Combs collection.*
Row 4, Right	BROOCH	1960	**Kramer.** Multi-color rhinestones and aurora borealis stones in filigree mounting. *Lynn Warech collection.*
Bottom Row	EARRINGS	1950-60	**Weiss.** Japanned mounting for Austrian *faux* gemstones. *Mildred Combs collection.*

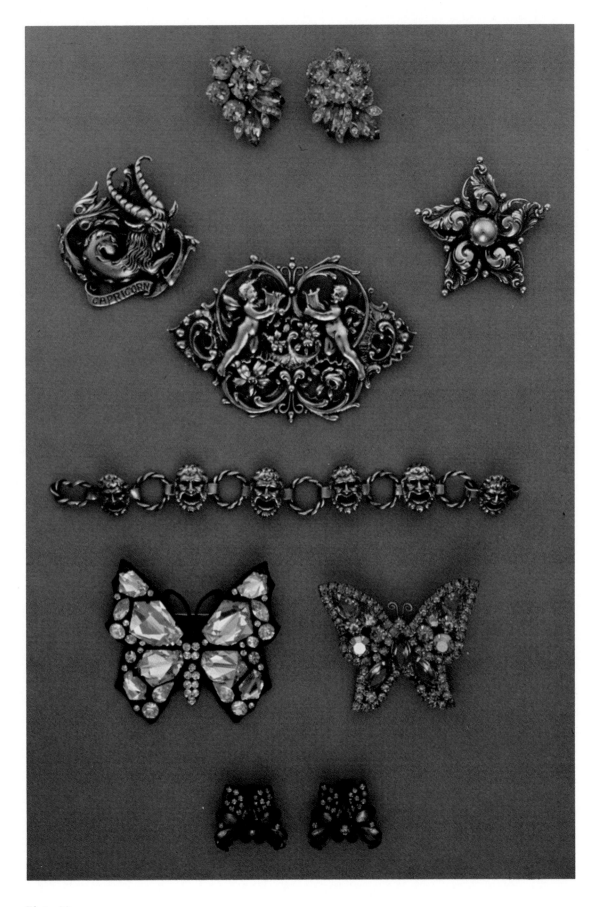

Plate 30.

Plate 31

Location	Nomenclature	Circa	Description
Top	Set: EARRINGS & PENDANT-NECKLACE	1960	**Unmarked.** Heavy gold electroplating. Prong-set Czechoslovakia *faux* turquoise and rubies. Exquisite workmanship. *Lynn Warech collection.*
Center	PENDANT	1948	**Marked "Czech".** Antiqued gilded brass, set with *faux* turquoise and garnets. Renaissance design influence. *Author's collection.*
Bottom	NECKLACE	1925	**Unmarked.** Gilt and enamel filigree, with Venetian ruby color glass beads. *Author's collection.*

Plate 31.

Plate 32

Location	Nomenclature	Circa	Description
Top, Left	EARRINGS	1950-55	**Renoir.** Copper wrought in Art Moderne design. Clip-type earrings.
Top, Right	EARRINGS	1950-55	**Renoir.** Enamel on copper. Art Moderne design influence. Clip-on earrings.
Row 2	BRACELET	1950-55	**Renoir.** Copper handwrought in link-type bracelet. Art Moderne.
Center	EARRINGS	1950	**Renoir.** Copper, clip-type earrings.
Bottom	NECKLACE	1935-40	**Gray Kingsbury, N.Y.** - Antiqued brass, Egyptian motifs, with cinnabar beads utilized as pendants. Matching bracelet not shown. *Veronica Newell collection.*

Plate 32.
Allison Dickason collection unless otherwise noted.

Plate 33

Location	Nomenclature	Circa	Description
Top, L - R	PIN	1950-60	**Weiss.** Figural butterfly. Multi-color *faux* gemstones. *Mildred Combs collection.*
	EARRINGS	1950	**Charel.** Foiled and faceted aurora borealis stones. *Allison Dickason collection.*
	PIN	1950-60	**Weiss.** Faceted, prong-set imitation gemstones. *Mildred Combs collection.*
Row 2, L - R & Bottom Row	Set: EARRINGS & BRACELET	1950	**Trifari.** *Faux* emeralds and peridot. Designed with aurora borealis center stones. *Mildred Combs collection.*
	Set: EARRINGS & BRACELET	1955-60	**Weiss.** Prong-set aurora borealis. *Allison Dickason collection.*
	Set: EARRINGS & BRACELET	1960	**Regency.** Japanned mounting with multi-color blue simulated stones. *Mildred Combs collection.*

Plate 33.

Plate 34

Location	Nomenclature	Circa	Description
Top	*PARURE:* Earrings, Brooch & Bracelet	1950	**Kramer.** Earrings, brooch and bracelet in tri-color *faux* gemstones. *Allison Dickason collection.*
Center	NECKLACE	1960	**Napier.** Flexible links, silver finish, adjustable chain. Art Moderne design. *Jenny Biddle collection.*
Center	EARRINGS	1950	**Renoir.** Etched and engraved clip-type. Copper. *Peggy Covey collection.*
Bottom, Left	BROOCH	1950	**Kramer.** Multi-color, faceted stones. *Allison Dickason collection.*
Bottom, Right	PIN	1960	**Castlecliff.** Simulated stones in gilded metal. *Jenny Biddle collection.*

Plate 34.

Plate 35

Location	Nomenclature	Circa	Description
Top	PIN	1945-50	**Miriam Haskell.** Movable tassels. Gilded brass.
Center	EARRINGS	1955	**Mosell.** Foiled glass cabachons set in gilded brass.
Center to Bottom	NECKLACE	1955	**Goldette.** Cast and molded Egyptian motifs, with agate gemstone beads.

Plate 35.
Mildred Combs collection.

Plate 36

Location	Nomenclature	Circa	Description
Row 1, Left	PIN	1970	**Emmons. "Tinlizzy".** Rhodium and rhinestones. *Author's collection.*
Row 1, Right	EARRINGS	1950	**Eisenberg.** Rhodium, set with pear-shape, marquis cut and roundels of prong-set rhinestones. Clip earring. *Author's collection.*
Row 2	BRACELET	1945-50	**Unmarked.** (Possibly Eisenberg). Rhodium, set with marquis cut petals and other faceted and prong-set rhinestones. Flexible links and heavy banding on reverse side. *Author's collection.*
Row 3	BRACELET	1948-50	**Kramer of New York.** Rhodium, flexible cuff bracelet. Individually cupped and prong-set finest quality rhinestones. *Author's collection.*
Row 4, Left	Pair: DRESS CLIPS	1933	**Marked: "1933 copyright".** Manufacturer not identified. Rhinestones in white metal, with claw-set *faux* sapphires. *Mary Ruth Evry collection.*
Row 4, Right	BROOCH	1950	**Eisenberg.** Rhodium, with emerald cut and round rhinestones. *Author's collection.*
Row 5	BRACELET	1955	**Weiss.** Flexible rhodium, with prong-set pear-shape, round and emerald cut rhinestones. All accentuated by marquis cut fine rhinestones. *Lynn Warech collection.*
Row 6, Left	EARRINGS	1950	**Trifari.** Apple design. Rhodium, with baquette cut rhinestones. Clip earrings. *Author's collection.*
Row 6, Right	Set: PIN & EARRINGS	1950	**Trifari.** Rhodium, with *pave'* set rhinestones and emerald-cut stones tracing outline of leaves. Clip earrings. *Author's collection.*

Plate 36.

Plate 37

Location	Nomenclature	Circa	Description
Top, L - R	SCARF PIN	1950	**Standard.** Rhinestones in rhodium. *Allison Dickason collection.*
	EARRINGS	1955	**Pen'n. (Pennino)** Multi-faceted rhinestones. *Mildred Combs collection.*
	PIN	1948-50	**Kramer of N.Y.** - Rhinestones and cultured pearls. *Mildred Combs collection.*
	FUR CLIP	1940	**Trifari.** Faceted rhinestones in sterling silver. *Mildred Combs collection.*
Center	BROOCH	1930	**Eisenberg.** Sterling figural butterfly. Exceptionally large brooch is set with *faux* gemstones. Fine pierced mounting. *Mildred Combs collection.*
Bottom, Left	EARRINGS	1955-65	**Panetta.** Rhodium and rhinestone. *Allison Dickason collection.*
Bottom, Center	PENDANT-NECKLACE	1930	**Trifari.** Art Moderne design. Black glass and rhinestones set in white metal. (Design now being reproduced in 1970-1980 in composition plastic.) *Mildred Combs collection.*
Bottom, Right	PIN	1960	**Boucher.** Rhodium, with *pave'* set baquette cut rhinestones. *Allison Dickason collection.*

Plate 37.

Plate 38

Location	Nomenclature	Circa	Description
Top Left	EARRINGS	1940	**Marked: "Pat. Sterling"**. Handwrought sterling, set with polished agate. Clip earrings.
Top, Right	PIN	1935	**Unmarked**. Art Moderne, figural bird in flight. Combination of polished wood and carved translucent plastic.
Center	EARRINGS	1950	**Trifari**. Rhodium cast in Art Moderne motif. Clip earrings.
Center	NECKLACE	1950	**Monet**. Rhodium linked, choker length necklace, Art Moderne styling.
Bottom, Left	BROOCH	1940	**Unmarked**. German silver, with *faux plique-a-jour* work done in plastic rather than enamelling. Accented with marcasites. Transitional *nouveau* style to "depression expression deco".
Bottom, Right	SCARF PIN	1950	**Emmons**. Rhodium tassels and pin. Reproduced from a mid-Victorian era scarf pin.

Plate 38.
Author's collection.

Plate 39

Location	Nomenclature	Circa	Description
Row 1	EARRINGS	1945	**Trifari.** Enamel and rhinestones, set in rhodium. Clip-type. *Jean Wise collection.*
Row 2	BRACELET	1945	**Trifari.** Rhodium with painted enamelling, set with rhinestones and *faux* ruby. *Jean Wise collection.*
Center	BROOCH	1960	**Trifari.** Crown design, set with cabachon *faux* gemstones and faceted rhinestones. *Mary Ruth Evry collection.*
Bottom	NECKLACE	1950	**Trifari.** Goldtone set with *pave'* rhinestones and *faux* sapphires. Beautiful baroque influence in designing. *Mary Ruth Evry collection.*

Plate 39.

Plate 40

Location	Nomenclature	Circa	Description
Top, Left	BROOCH	1960	**Castlecliff.** Pink baroque pearl set in heavy gold electroplate. Branch coral design.
Top, Right	PIN	1950	**Kramer.** Wired simulated pearls, set in gold electroplate.
Center Row, Left	PIN	1950	**Authentic/Vans.** Prong-set rhinestones given a hint of smoky color.
Center Row, Middle	COMPACT	1950	**Elgin American.** Designed and signed by **Salvadore Dali.** (See Plate 41 for signature). Head of bird is a **lipstick.** Wings spread to reveal a **powder compact.** Tail pulls out, and contains a **pillbox.** Unmarked metallic content. **Dali's** signature elevates value.
Center Row, Right	PIN	1940	**Accessocraft.** Gold electroplate. Maltese cross design. Etruscan influence.
Bottom, Left	EARRINGS	1950	**Napier.** Rope design in gold electroplate.
Bottom, Right	PIN	1955	**Cadoro.** Double bow, goldtone. Ideal scarf pin.

Plate 40.
Janet St.Amant collection.

Plate 41

Location	Nomenclature	Circa	Description
Top, Left	PIN	1955	**Original by Robért.** Enamelling on gold electroplate, with pearl accent.
Top, Right	BROOCH	1955	**Jomaz.** Exquisitely cast design, set with rhinestones and *faux* emerald.
Center, Left	COMPACT	1950	**Elgin American.** Designed by Dali. (Note signature). Details on Plate 40, which shows obverse side.
Center, Right	Set: PIN & EARRINGS	1960	**Boucher.** *Faux* turquoise cabachons set in gold electroplate.
Bottom, Left	PIN	1960	**DeNicola.** Goldtone filigree design, set with rhinestones and pink quartz.
Bottom, Right	BRACELET	1965-70	**Cadora.** Gold electroplate, set with *Faux* emeralds and turquoise.

Plate 41.
Janet St.Amant collection.

Plate 42

Location	Nomenclature	Circa	Description
Top, L - R	PIN	1960	**Weiss.** Christmas Tree design, highlighted with multi-color faceted stones. *Author's collection.*
	PIN	1955	**BSK.** Pearl and multi-color stones. *Allison Dickason collection.*
	PIN	1960	**Dalsheim.** Novelty pin, painted enamelling on goldtone. *Allison Dickason collection.*
Row 2, L - R	PIN	1960	**Coro.** Foiled *faux* topaz color faceted stones, paste-set in mold. *Allison Dickason collection.*
	EARRINGS	1965	**Weiss.** Faceted stones, prong-set in clip-style goldtone earrings. *Allison Dickason collection.*
	PIN	1960	**Vendome.** Enamelling on goldtone, with faceted prong-set topaz color rhinestones. (Matching earrings not shown). *Author's collection.*
Row 3, L - R	EARRINGS	1960	**Hollycraft.** Pastel colors in faceted stones set in goldtone. Clip earrings. *Mildred Combs collection.*
	PIN	1955	**Trifari.** Goldtone flower design, set with aurora borealis stones. *Allison Dickason collection.*
	EARRINGS	1965	**Astra.** Pasted, foiled multi-color stones. *Allison Dickason collection.*
Row 4, L - R	PIN	1965	**Sarah Coventry.** Large, green glass stones set in goldtone. Filigreee cups for sets, including small green accents. *Author's collection.*
	PIN	1960	**BSK.** Aurora borealis paste-mounted stones set in goldtone. *Allison Dickason collection.*
	KILT PIN	1965	**Miracle.** Reproduction of antique design. Burnished goldtone w/*faux* stones and enamelling. *Allison Dickason collection.*

Plate 42.

Plate 43

Location	Nomenclature	Circa	Description
Top, Left & Center	Set: EARRINGS & NECKLACE	1955-60	**Trifari.** White glass beads with gilded filigree leaf accents.
Top, Center	PIN	1955-60	**Trifari.** Goldtone, set with composition turquoise color stones.
Top, Right	PIN	1955-60	**Trifari.** Enamelled goldtone.
Center	BROOCH	1955-60	**Trifari.** Enamelled white glass.
Bottom	Set: BRACELET & EARRINGS	1955-60	**Trifari.** White enamelling, and turquoise blue composition stones set in gold electroplate, cast mounting.

Plate 43.
Allison Dickason collection.

Plate 44

Location	Nomenclature	Circa	Description
Top, Left	Set: NECKLACE & DROP EARRINGS	1950	**Mosell.** Gilt, with simulated stones. Pendant-type drop earrings and necklace, show Etruscan period design influence.
Top, Right	PIN	1960	**ABC, Inc.** Painted enamel. Art Moderne design.
Center and Bottom	Set: BRACELET & NECKLACE	1950	**Mosell.** Simulated turquoise and rhinestones set in gilded, finely linked brass. (Replica of earlier **c.** 1925 jewelry, showing Egyptian influence design).
Bottom, Center	PIN	1955-65	**Brooks.** Gilded brass, with rhinestone accents. Figural bird in flight.

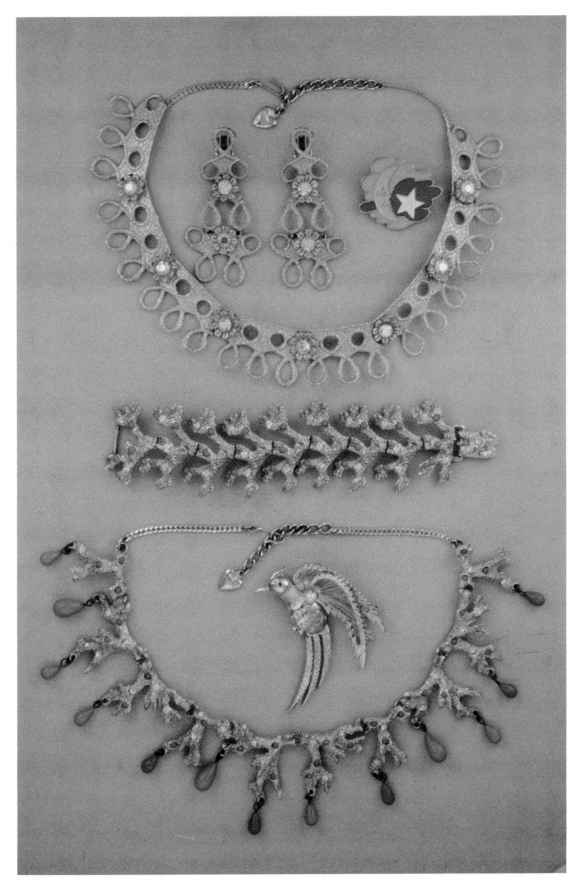

Plate 44.
Mildred Combs collection.

Plate 45

Location	Nomenclature	Circa	Description
Top	PIN	1950	**Miriam Haskell.** Emerald-cut and round rhinestones, finely set in a gilt mounting.
Left	BRACELET	1950	**Napier.** Gold electroplated flexible mesh, with clasp rendered in molded *faux* jade.
Row 2, L - R	PIN	1960	**LesBernard, Inc.** - *Pave'* set rhinestones and simulated pearl, in gilded mounting.
	PIN	1950	**Miriam Haskell.** Burnished gilt mounting. Seed pearls accent rhinestones, plus a large baroque wax-bead pearl.
Row 3, L - R	PIN	1950	**Miriam Haskell.** Symmetrical antiqued gilt mount, set with seed pearls and simulated large center pearl.
	PIN	1960	**DeMario, N.Y.** - Gilded mounting, set with pearls and rhinestones. (Note similarity of design compared to **Miriam Haskell** jewelry).
Bottom	PIN	1950	**Miriam Haskell.** Antiqued gilded mount, set with simulated pearls.

Plate 45.
Mary Ruth Evry collection.

Plate 46

Location	Nomenclature	Circa	Description
Top, L - R	PIN	1945-50	**Cini for Gumps.** (Gumps, San Francisco) Sterling figural floral, handcrafted. *Mildred Combs collection.*
	BROOCH	1950-60	**Hobé.** Sterling, with loop for pendant chain. Handcrafted. *Allison Dickason collection.*
	PIN	1945-50	**Theda.** Antiqued sterling, florentine finish. Set with *faux* green and blue stone accents in tailfeathers. Red stones in crown. Fine figural Peacock. *Mildred Combs collection.*
Row 2	BRACELET	1940	**JewelArt.** Sterling, with finely engraved charm. *Allison Dickason collection.*
Row 3, L - R	PIN	1945-50	**Guillermo Cini.** Sterling *repousse. Mildred Combs collection.*
	PIN	1940	**Korda. "Thief of Bagdad".** Filigree with figural "magical lamp", and a pendant in shape of an Egyptian mummy case. Korda was film's producer. This pin could possibly be a souvenir or commemorative of film's release in 1940. *Mildred Combs collection.*
	PIN	1950-60	**Cini.** Stunning sterling silver filigree, **"St. George slaying the dragon"** motif. *Mildred Combs collection.*
Row 4, L - R	PENDANT	1950	**J.J.** - Pewter, with moveable goldtone spectacles worn by figural bunny. Small loop on pendant, for chain. *Allison Dickason collection.*
	PIN	1950-60	**Danecraft.** Sterling charm or pendant. Shamrock, w/sterling hallmarked casing. *Allison Dickason collection.*
	PIN	1950	**Beau.** Sterling, Art Moderne designed figural cat. *Allison Dickason collection.*

Plate 46.

Plate 47

Location	Nomenclature	Circa	Description
Top, L - R	PIN	1950	**B.S.K.** - Goldtone, with *faux* ruby gemstone accents.
	PIN	1950	**Polcini.** Painted enamel on goldtone, with movable limbs.
	PIN	1960-65	**B.S.K.** - **"My Fair Lady"**. Goldtone, set with imitation stones.
Row 2, L - R	PIN	1950-60	**Park Lane.** Two-tone florentine or brushed antiqued finish, with goldtone accents.
	BROOCH	1970	**Tortolani.** Crown design with simulated pearls.
	PIN	1960	**J.J.** - Goldtone, **"Mouse on Ice Skates"**. Wind-swept scarf provides action, and is highlighted by painted enamelling. One of many popular "scatter" pins in sixties.
Row 3, L - R	PIN	1960	**Gerry's.** Woodland creature in goldtone.
	PIN	1965-70	**Karu 5th Ave.** - Rabbit, painted enamel tongue. *Faux* emerald eyes, and rhinestone accents.
	PIN	1960	**Manolf.** Goldtone figural lion, with stone accents. Another "scatter" pin.
Bottom, L - R	PIN	1960	**B.S.K.** - Cast goldtone figural lion. *Mildred Combs collection.*
	PIN	1965	**Schreiner.** Figural turtle with prong-set large pearl body and imitation prong-set stones. Head on a spring.
	PIN	1960	**B.S.K.** - Goldtone, hand cast figural cat. *Mildred Combs collection.*

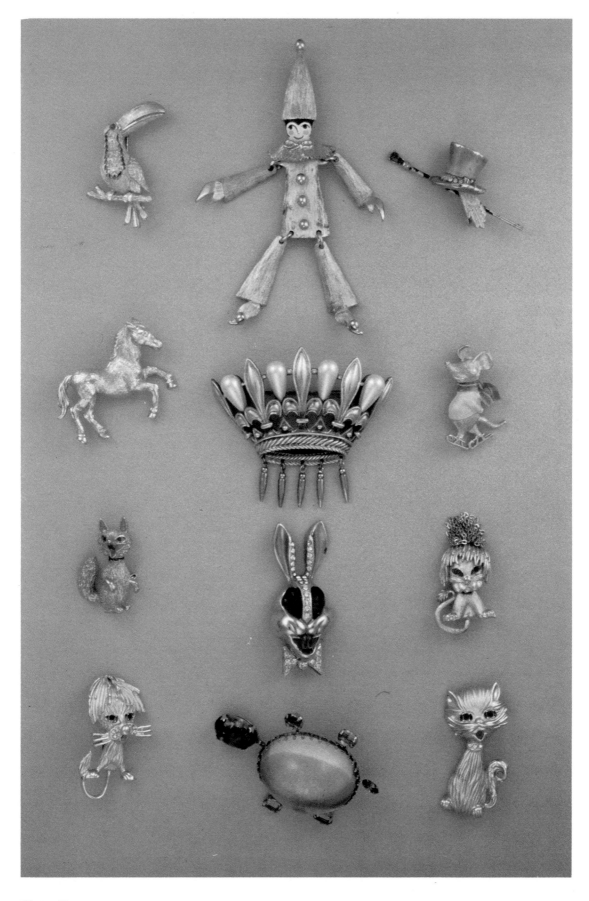

Plate 47.
Allison Dickason collection unless otherwise noted.

Plate 48

Location	Nomenclature	Circa	Description
Top, Left	Set: PIN & EARRINGS	1950-60	**Eisenberg.** Multi-color amethyst faceted glass stones, and brilliant rhinestones set in rhodium. *Annette Harrelson collection.*
Top, Right	PIN	1960	**Weisner.** Imitation sapphires with *pave'* set rhinestones. *Allison Dickason collection.*
Row 2, Left	PIN	1950	**Trifari.** Rhodium *Fleur-de-Lis* with cultured pearls. *Author's collection.*
Row 2, Right	Set: EARRINGS & PIN	1950-60	**Trifari.** Rhodium set with large cultured pearls. *Virginia McCurdy collection.*
Row 3	Set: EARRINGS & PIN	1960	**Eisenberg Ice.** Blue and Green imitation faceted stones, prong-set combined with Austrian rhinestones. *Annette Harrelson collection.*
Row 4, L - R	PIN	1960	**Trifari.** Rose-cut rhinestones in rhodium. *Allison Dickason collection.*
	PIN	1960	**Marvella.** Simulated pearls and rhinestones set in rhodium. *Allison Dickason collection.*
	PIN	1960	**Trifari.** Finely cut baquette and *pave'* set rhinestones. *Allison Dickason collection.*

Plate 48.

Plate 49

Location	Nomenclature	Circa	Description
Top, Center	PIN	1955	**Miriam Haskell.** Filigree and fretwork in goldtone. Set with seed pearls and large center pearl.
Top, Left and Right	SCARF PINS	1955	**Miriam Haskell.** Two unique designs, utilizing various size pearls. Note how the safety nibs complement the overall designs of the top ornaments.
Center	BROOCH	1955	**Miriam Haskell.** Exceptionally large, typical **Haskell** design, utilizing varied sizes of pearls. Note the galaxy of seed pearls, all in gilt wire mounting.
Bottom	Set: NECKLACE & EARRINGS	1955-65	**Kramer.** Wired pearls with multi chains linked in stylized manner. Also note the similarity to other jewelry on this Plate. **Miriam Haskell** pioneered the designs first conceived in the late thirties and early forties, highly popular in the fifties and sixties. Other fashion jewelry designers offered many variations on the jewelry themes introduced by **Miriam Haskell.**

Plate 49.
Allison Dickason collection.

Plate 50

Location	Nomenclature	Circa	Description
Top, L - R	PIN	1960-65	**Kramer.** Simulated, pressed pattern glass in gold electroplate. *Allison Dickason collection.*
	PIN	1965-70	**Hattie Carnegie.** *Faux* coral and turquoise, with rhinestones and seed pearls, in gold electroplate. (Copy from Tiffany & Co. design, made in 14K gold, and genuine gems.)
	PIN	1965-70	**Hattie Carnegie.** Imitation stones, combined with imitation horn. (Possibly another copy of Tiffany genre of jewelry, in gold and gems.).
Row 2, L - R	EARRINGS	1950-60	**Weiss.** Rhinestone and imitation turquoise stones. Clip-type earrings.
	Set: PIN & EARRINGS	1960	**Jomaz.** Deep green glass cabachons, prong-set with *faux* Persian turquoise and exquisitely impressive setting of *pave'* rhinestones.
	EARRINGS	1960	**Trifari.** *Faux* Persian turquoise cabachons, set in goldtone.
Row 3 & 4	Set: BRACELET & EARRINGS	1955-65	**Trifari.** "Jewels of India" production. Cultured pearls with rhinestones and *faux* turquoise cabachons.

Plate 50.
Mildred Combs collection unless otherwise noted.

Plate 51

Location	Nomenclature	Circa	Description
Left to Right	BRACELET	1950	**Emmons. "Rustic Beauty".** Antiqued goldtone replica of Georgian genre of jewelry. Set with rhinestones. (Pendant and earrings made to match).
	BRACELET	1970	**Emmons. "Coins of the Realm".** Hostess gift only. Patented goldtone. (Disc belt and earrings not shown).
	BRACELET	1970	**Emmons. "Scimitar".** Antiqued goldtone set with *faux* gemstones and simulated pearls as spacers. (Replica of fashionable jewelry **circa 1910** slides for chains.)
	BRACELET	1976	**Emmons. "Cleopatra Egyptian Queen".** Royal hostess gift. Oxidized goldtone, set with imitation stones. (Necklace and earrings not shown.)
Top, Right	PIN	1967	**Emmons. "Glamour-Puss".** Art Moderne cat with simulated stone eyes.
Bottom, Right	PIN	1960	**Emmons. "Scarecrow".** Goldtone "scatter" pin, with simulated pearl. Moveable "straw" tassle-like limbs.

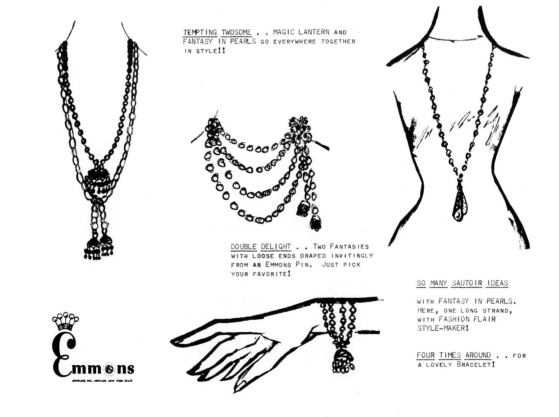

TEMPTING TWOSOME . . MAGIC LANTERN AND FANTASY IN PEARLS GO EVERYWHERE TOGETHER IN STYLE!!

DOUBLE DELIGHT . . TWO FANTASIES WITH LOOSE ENDS DRAPED INVITINGLY FROM AN EMMONS PIN. JUST PICK YOUR FAVORITE!

SO MANY SAUTOIR IDEAS

WITH FANTASY IN PEARLS. HERE, ONE LONG STRAND, WITH FASHION FLAIR STYLE-MAKER!

FOUR TIMES AROUND . . FOR A LOVELY BRACELET!

Emmons
JEWELERS INC., NEWARK, NEW YORK STATE

Credit: Eleanor Musser Archives

Plate 51.
Elaine Dill collection.

Plate 52

Location	Nomenclature	Circa	Description
Top	PIN	1940	**Danecraft.** Sterling *repousse. Allison Dickason collection.*
Center	EARRINGS	1950-60	**Castlecliff.** Rhodium. Finely cast pierce work. *Mildred Combs collection.*
	BUCKLE or SCARF PIN	1930	**H.Fargo.** Sterling buckle for hat or belt or could be used as scarf pin. *Allison Dickason collection.*
	NECKLACE or CHOKER	1940	**Danecraft.** Sterling. Cast design. (Choker with chain extender added for sizing.) *Mildred Combs collection.*
Bottom	BRACELET	1940	**Beau.** Sterling, etched and engraved. *Allison Dickason collection.*
	BROOCH	1950	**Danecraft.** Sterling *repousse,* with openwork and beading. *Allison Dickason collection.*

Plate 52.

Plate 53

Location	Nomenclature	Circa	Description
Top, Left	PIN	1955-65	**Hollycraft.** Christmas Tree design set with *faux* gemstones.
Top, Right	EARRINGS	1970-75	**Alice Caviness.** Wired beads on clip mounting.
Center	EARRINGS	1965-75	**Napier.** Beautifully engraved filigree mounting for prong-set gemstones.
	BEADED NECKLACE	1965-75	**DeMario.** Aurora borealis stones and tri-color amythest beads.
Bottom, Left	EARRINGS	1960-65	**Weiss.** Goldtone, set with multicolor imitation gemstones and aurora borealis stones.
Bottom, Right	EARRINGS	1960	**Robért.** Seed pearls with aurora borealis stones.

Plate 53.
Allison Dickason collection.

Plate 54

Location	Nomenclature	Circa	Description
Top	BRACELET	1950	**Coro.** Gold electroplated set with aurora borealis stones. Art Moderne influence. *Bonnie Brown collection.*
Center	PIN	1950	**Weiss.** Multi-colored faceted Bohemian glass stones set in oxidized mounting. *Author's collection.*
Bottom	Set: EARRINGS & NECKLACE	1955	**Vendome.** Iridescent bugle beads with multi-color faceted crystals, aurora borealis stones, and opaque roundels. Note unusual clasp, set with *faux* emeralds. Adjustable screw-clip earrings. Finely strung beads. *Author's collection.*

Plate 54.

Plate 55

Location	Nomenclature	Circa	Description
Top, L - R	PIN	1960-65	**Coro.** Goldtone floral with rhinestones. *Allison Dickason collection.*
	EARRINGS	1960	**Trifari.** Goldtone with rhinestones. *Mildred Combs collection.*
	PIN	1960	**Reia.** *Pave'* set rhinestones in goldtone. *Allison Dickason collection.*
Center	PIN	1950-55	**Coro.** Figural eagle in burnished goldtone mounting. *Mildred Combs collection.*
	NECKLACE	1945	**Monet.** Goldtone, heavy cast linkage. *Allison Dickason collection.*
Bottom, L - R	FUR CLIP	1945-55	**Trifari.** *Pave'* set rhinestones in *vermeil,* (gold wash over sterling silver). *Mildred Combs collection.*
	EARRINGS	1965	**Christian Dior.** Shell design, in gold electroplate. *Allison Dickason collection.*
	PIN	1950-60	**Jeanne.** Heavy cast, burnished goldtone. Fine hand stipling work. *Mildred Combs collection.*

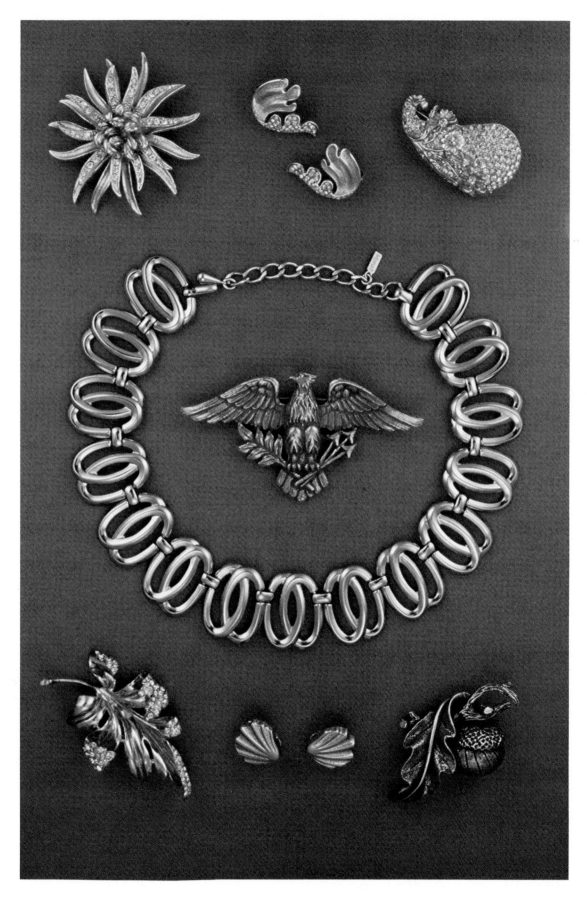

Plate 55.

Plate B-1 (Opposite Page)

Location	Nomenclature	Circa	Description
Top	Set: EARRINGS & NECKLACE	1940-50	**Miriam Haskell.** Champagne color simulated pearls with rhinestones, in filigree gilt mounting.
Bottom, Center	PIN	1940-50	**Miriam Haskell.** Crystal beads and rhinestones in filigree antiqued gilt mounting.
Bottom	NECKLACE	1940-50	**Miriam Haskell.** Crystals and rhinestones in choker style necklace. Rhinestones are individually linked and flexible on this gilt chain collar.

Plate D-1 (Below)

Left: Hat Ornament, c. 1930-1940. Large faceted rhinestones in silver metal. Unmarked.

Center: Hat Ornament, c. 1940-1950. Lady Bug figural, set with *pave'* rhinestones. Painted enamel body and red glass eye accents.

Right: Hat Ornament, c. 1925-1930. Art Deco. Channel-set rhinestones in silver metal. Probably lead base metal, making ornament quite heavy.

The "nibs" on hat ornaments shown right and left, carry out the design of the ornamental heads.

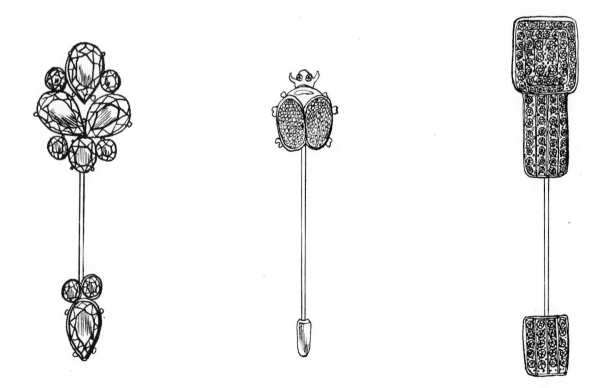

Drawings: Joyce Fairchild. Author's collection.
(Previously published in Lillian Baker's, *Collector's Encyclopedia of Hatpins and Hatpin Holders*, Collector Books, 1978).

Plate B-1.
Sharry Clark Collection.
Photo Credit: Dave Hammell

Plate B-2 (Opposite Page)

Location	Nomenclature	Circa	Description
Top, Left	PIN	1960	**Original by Robért.** Simulated pearls and rhinestones in floral design. Wire and open work gilded mounting.
Top, Right	PIN	1940	**Miriam Haskell.** Simulated pearls and *pave'* set rhinestones in tri-dimensional gilded mounting.
Center	PIN	1935-40	**Miriam Haskell.** Inspired by Victorian style bar pin. Pearls and rhinestones set in filigree mounting.
Bottom, Center	PIN	1960	©**Original by Robért.** Wired beads, painted enamel and rhinestones set in an engraved Victorian type mounting.
Bottom	NECKLACE	1950	**Miriam Haskell.** Champagne color simulated pearls set with *pave'* rhinestone drops. Unique and exquisite fashion piece. Note graduated sizes of pearls.

Plate B-2.
Sharry Clark Collection.
Photo Credit: Dave Hammell

Plate B-3 (Opposite Page)

Location	Nomenclature	Circa	Description
Top Row, L-R	PIN	1945-60	**Miriam Haskell.** Blue glass *faux* lapis cabachons and rhinestones set in open filigree mounting.
	EARRINGS	1970	**Kenneth Lane®** . Channel set rhinestones with large pearl.
	PIN	1965	**DeMario, N.Y.** Filigree floral with heart-shaped faceted crystals. *Faux* Persian turquoise cabachons and rhinestones.
Row 2	Set: PIN & EARRINGS	1955-65	**Regency.** Wax bead pearls with varied shapes of faceted rhinestones.
Row 3, Left	PIN	1965-70	**Regency.** Simulated pearls and rhinestones in floral design. Wire filigree.
Row 3, Right	PIN	1940-50	**Miriam Haskell.** Burnished gilt mounting. Prong-set, multiple-sized and cut fine rhinestones.
Bottom	Set: EARRINGS & NECKLACE	1970-75	**Alice Caviness.** Aurora borealis stones, with Austrian crystals and beads. Flexible rhinestone chain.

Plate B-3.
Sharry Clark Collection.
Photo Credit: Dave Hammell

Plate B-4 (Opposite Page)

Location	Nomenclature	Circa	Description
Left, Top to Bottom	SCARF PIN	1950-60	**Stanley Hagler.** Filigree mounting, set with simulated pearls, faceted rhinestones, and *faux* gem accents.
	PIN	1965-70	**Hattie Carnegie.** *Pave'* rhinestones set in burnished antiqued silver color mounting
	PIN	1950-60	**Kramer of N.Y.** Japanned metal with faceted and prong-set rhinestones.
	PIN	1940-50	**Miriam Haskell.** Oxidized metal set with rhinestones.
Right	BRACELET	1965-75	**Original by Robért.** Flexible band set with simulated pearls, blue and crystal beads, rhinestones and four simulated moonstones.

Plate D-2 (Below)

Left: Hatpin, c. 1925-1935. Beads and sequins hand sewn on black felt. Pin-stem measures 4½″. Color of sequins and beads usually complemented hat or accessories.

Center: Hatpin, c. 1925-1935. Art Deco black plastic feather shape, mounted in a gilded metallic wire-work, accented by two rhinestones. Pin-stem measures 5″.

Right: Hatpin, c. 1935-1940. Wax-bead baroque shape pearl, with silver base metal disc set with rhinestones. Pin-stem measures 6½″.

Hatpins made for the masses, were generally unmarked, as are these.

Drawings: Joyce Fairchild. Author's collection.
(Previously published in Lillian Baker's, *Collector's Encyclopedia of Hatpins and Hatpin Holders*, Collector Books, 1978).

Plate B-4.
Sharry Clark Collection.
Photo Credit: Dave Hammell

Plate B-5 (Opposite Page)

Location	Nomenclature	Circa	Description
Top	Set: EARRINGS & NECKLACE	1950-60	**Eugene.** Pink and crystal beads with translucent glass flower petals, accented with bugle beads and rhinestones.
Bottom	*PARURE:* Ring, pendant-necklace & pendant-ear-rings	1945-50	**Miriam Haskell.** Rare molded, varigated color resin cameos, gypsy mounted in antiqued frames accented with bugle beads. Workmanship and color of plastic seeks to imitate the natural colors of conch shells ordinarily used for carved cameos. Unusual **Miriam Haskell** jewelry conception.

Plate D-3 (Below)

Hat Ornaments, (Left to Right). All are c. 1925-1940.

Black glass beads, sewn on felt cotton-stuffed form, mounted into a silver color metallic ring studded with rhinestones. A wax-bead pearl garishly holds this assemblege atop a 3½" pin-stem. Threaded metallic pointed nib, holds the hat ornament in place, once it is inserted and positioned on the hat.

Multiple color iridescent beads combined with rhinestones. Matched wax-bead pearls attach the "blob" to top of pin, and its counterpart forms a nib with cork insert to hold pin securely.

Two "French Ivory" plastic Art Deco heads and free-form nibs.

Highly iridescent imitation pearls are set on either side of oxidized silver color metal with hammered leaf motif. Very well made.

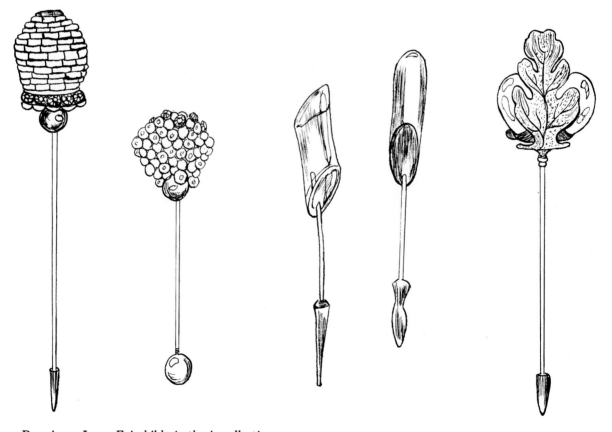

Drawings: Joyce Fairchild. Author's collection.
(Previously published in Lillian Baker's, *Collector's Encyclopedia of Hatpins and Hatpin Holders*, Collector Books, 1978).

Plate B-5.
Sharry Clark Collection.
Photo Credit: Dave Hammell

Plate B-6 (Opposite Page)

Location	Nomenclature	Circa	Description
Top	HAIR ORNAMENT	1940-50	**Miriam Haskell.** Floral wire-work with metallic bead dangles on simulated tortoise hair pin.
Center	SIDE COMBS	1940-50	**Miriam Haskell.** Pair of simulated tortoise with fine filigree metallic mounts for rhinestones and wire-mounted large wax pearl beads. (Popularized by Betty Grable's upswept hair style shown on "Pin-Up Girl" World War II poster.)
Bottom	PIN	1950-60	**Regency Jewels.** Cast mounting, set with aurora borealis stones.

Plate D-4 (Below)

Hat Ornaments, (Left to Right). All c. 1925-1935. Overall measurements, 6½″-7½″.

Sterling silver hat ornament, with flattened tip to slide into a slit of a felt hat. Although primarily an ornament, this particular pin could also serve to secure the hat more firmly to the head. Therefore, it could be either a hat ornament or a hatpin. Etched and engraved, marked "sterling".

Plastic ring is harnessed by goldtone metal which is studded with various sized rhinestones. Fanciful hat ornament, typical of the Art Deco and Art Moderne periods. Engraved metallic nib, matches the overall design of ornament.

Well-made cast metallic molded ornament, chased and engraved detail.

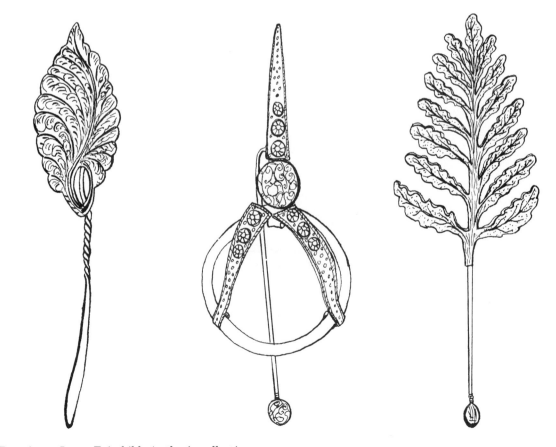

Drawings: Joyce Fairchild. Author's collection.
(Previously published in Lillian Baker's, *Collector's Encyclopedia of Hatpins and Hatpin Holders*, Collector Books, 1978).

Plate B-6.
Sharry Clark Collection.
Photo Credit: Dave Hammell

Plate B-7 (Opposite Page)

Location	Nomenclature	Circa	Description
Full Plate	Set: EARRINGS & NECKLACE	1935	**Unmarked.** Antiqued hammered, etched and engraved mounting. Imitation glass American turquoise matrix, amethysts and aquamarines. Copy of American Indian squash blossom design. German silver. Exquisite detail and workmanship, including all finely cut stones, prong-set.

Plate D-5 (Below)

Plastic Hatpins, c. 1930-1940

Three examples of free-form design manufactured in colored plastics of this period. Pin-stems measure 4½″-6″ and primarily these were utilized in the thirties and up through the early forties. The plastics were hand painted in varied colors of green, red, purple, yellow, orange and black. Unlike the more solid bakelite and later compostion plastics, these hatpins are crudely made, lightweight plastic just a step above the earlier produced celluloid. Most of these types of hatpins were not preserved because the need had expired and they were not easily stored in a bureau drawer. However, many survived stuck into the beaded pincushions, or half-doll pincushions. Plastic hat ornaments and hatpins are much sought after by collectors, who seek out the more bizarre shapes and blatant colorations.

Drawings: Joyce Fairchild. Author's collection.
(Previously published in Lillian Baker's, *Collector's Encyclopedia of Hatpins and Hatpin Holders*, Collector Books, 1978).

140

Plate B-7.
Nancy Franz Collection.
Photo Credit: Dave Hammell

Plate B-8(a) & B-8(b) (Opposite Page)

Location	Nomenclature	Circa	Description
Full Plate	CHOKER	1935	**Marked: "Pat.Pend."** Rhinestones set in rhodium plated white metal. Etched flexible neck-band. **Photo B-8(b)** shows unique fastening device.

Plate D-6 (Below)

An assortment of HAT ORNAMENTS with various shaped NIBS. Circa 1924-45. The Hat Ornaments are all in jeweler's "pot metal", pewter, nickle or other white alloys (silver-color).

Pearls, imitation moonstones, rhinestones, crystal, plastics and peking glass are represented here, including paste amethysts. All of the NIBS are threaded, except for the large round ornament. It has a plunger-type safety-nib.

The ornament with the pair of chicks is unusual and could have been made for a series of "little folk" hat ornaments, such as those worn in a beret or woolen cap.

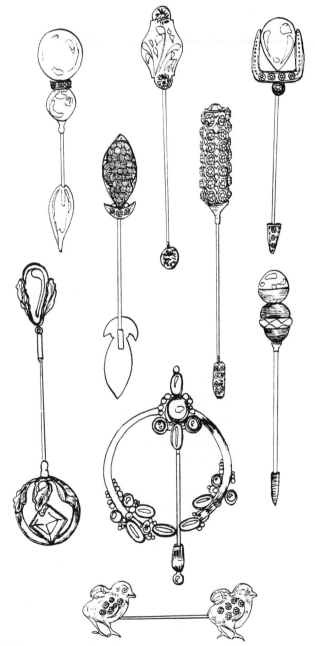

Drawings: Joyce Fairchild. Author's collection.
(Previously published in Lillian Baker's, *Collector's Encyclopedia of Hatpins and Hatpin Holders*, Collector Books, 1978).

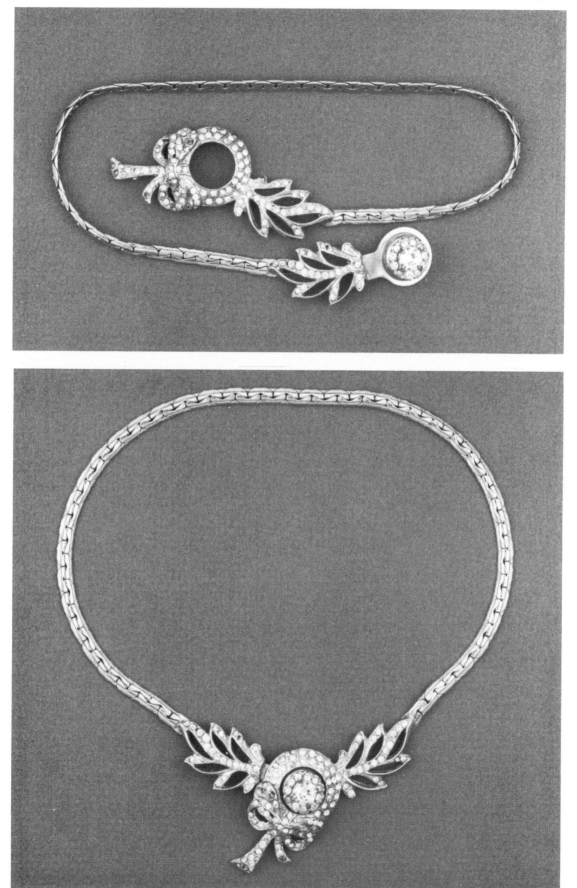

Plate B-8 (a) and (b).
Nancy Franz Collection.
Photo Credit: Dave Hammell

Plate B-9 (Below)

Location	Nomenclature	Circa	Description
Full Plate	BROOCH	1935	**Vogue**. Marked "Sterling". Unfoiled, faceted and *marquise* cut crystals. All prong-set. Open back, on a wire frame. Center set is a large emerald-cut *faux* aquamarine. A most impressive brooch.

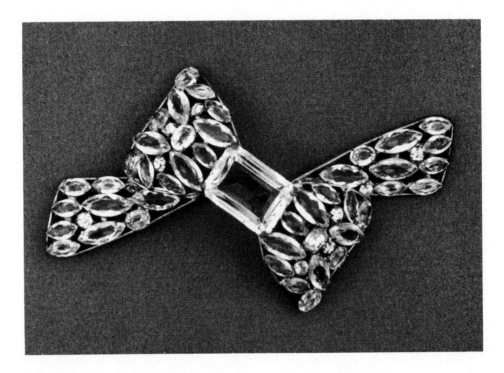

Plate B-9.
Nancy Franz Collection.
Photo Credit: Dave Hammell

Plate B-10 (Below)

Location	Nomenclature	Circa	Description
Top to Bottom	PINS	1950	**Trifari.** Bodies of molded acrylic, sterling silver and marcasites. Frog's eyes are colored glass molded cabachons.

Plate B-10.
Fred Silberman Collection.
Photo Credit: David Arky
From: *Art Plastic: Designed for Living* by Andrea DiNoto (See Bibliography)

Plate B-11 (Below)

Location	Nomenclature	Circa	Description
Full Plate	PENDANT	1965	**Hattie Carnegie.** Two inch pendant. Example of "Pop Art". Chrome plated sardine can, holds fish made of molded plastic.

Plate B-11.
Andrea DiNoto Collection.
Photo Credit: David Arky
From: *Art Plastic: Designed for Living* by Andrea DiNoto (See
    Bibliography)

Plate B-12 (Below)

Location	Nomenclature	Circa	Description
Full Plate	BRACELET	1930	**Unmarked.** Elasticized cuff bracelet. Large yellow phenolic resin rods and chunky green resin with metal bead spacers.

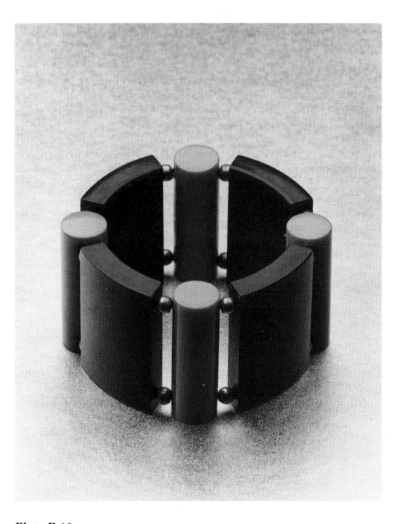

Plate B-12.
Susan Ellsworth Collection.
Photo Credit: David Arky
From: *Art Plastic: Designed for Living* by Andrea DiNoto (See
    Bibliography)

Plate B-13 (Below)

Location	Nomenclature	Circa	Description
Full Plate	BRACELETS & RING	1970	**Kenneth Jay Lane.** Assortment of high-fashion, uniquely designed pieces. Note the accent given to the variety of gorgeous clasps. This is a KJL trademark. Incorporated are *faux* cabachon gemstones. Forefinger rings were also popularized by K.J.L. **Jewelry featured in KJL ads.**

Plate B-13.
Photo Credit: Courtesy Kenneth Jay Lane

Plate B-14 (Below)

Location	Nomenclature	Circa	Description
Full Plate	EARRINGS & "DOG COLLAR"	1970	**Kenneth Jay Lane.** "Dog collar" type choker of small gilded beads on soft flex-chain. Exceptionally large drop earrings of faceted crystal and gilt. (Earrings also shown on Plate B-19).

Plate B-14.
Photo Credit: Courtesy Kenneth Jay Lane

Plate B-15 (Below)

Location	Nomenclature	Circa	Description
Full Plate	EARRINGS & CHOKER	1970	**Kenneth Jay Lane.** High rising evening choker of pearl and rhinestone, with dramatic matching shower-drop earrings. **KJL jewelry advertisement.**

Plate B-15.
Photo Credit: Courtesy Kenneth Jay Lane

Plate B-16 (Below)

Location	Nomenclature	Circa	Description
Full Plate	PENDANT-NECKLACE	1970	**Kenneth Jay Lane.** Heirloom necklace of jeweltone cabachons, set in gold links, with pendant of matrix turquoise cabachons and rhinestones. **KJL jewelry advertisement.**

Plate B-16.
Photo Credit: Courtesy Kenneth Jay Lane

Plate B-17 (Below)

Location	Nomenclature	Circa	Description
Full Plate	EARRINGS & NECKLACE	1970	**Kenneth Jay Lane.** Massive and marvelous design utilizing *faux* pearls and rhinestones.

Plate B-17.
Photo Credit: Courtesy Kenneth Jay Lane

Plate B-18 (Below)

Location	Nomenclature	Circa	Description
Full Plate	EARRINGS & NECKLACE	1971	**Kenneth Jay Lane.** Opulent bib necklace inspired by Oriental design. Carved jade outlines with rhinestones and complemented by drop earrings. **KJL advertisement.**

Plate B-18.
Photo Credit: Courtesy Kenneth Jay Lane

Plate B-19 (Below)

Location	Nomenclature	Circa	Description
Full Plate	EARRINGS & PENDANT-NECKLACE	1970	**Kenneth Jay Lane.** Drop earrings of faceted crystal and goldtone. Pendant necklace in a daring dimension, high fashion jewelry. Accented with crystals and *faux* gemstones. (Earrings also shown on Plate B-14). **KJL jewelry advertisements.**

Plate B-19.
Photo Credit: Courtesy Kenneth Jay Lane

Plate B-20 (Below)

Location	Nomenclature	Circa	Description
Top	PIN	1970	**Kenneth Jay Lane.** Maltese cross set with rhinestones in goldtone.
Bottom, L-R	4 Rings	1970	**Kenneth Jay Lane.** Cabachon crystals set in gold dome ring; single faceted crystal ball ring; unfaceted double crystal ball and rhinestone ring; and single unfaceted crystal ball and rhinestone ring.

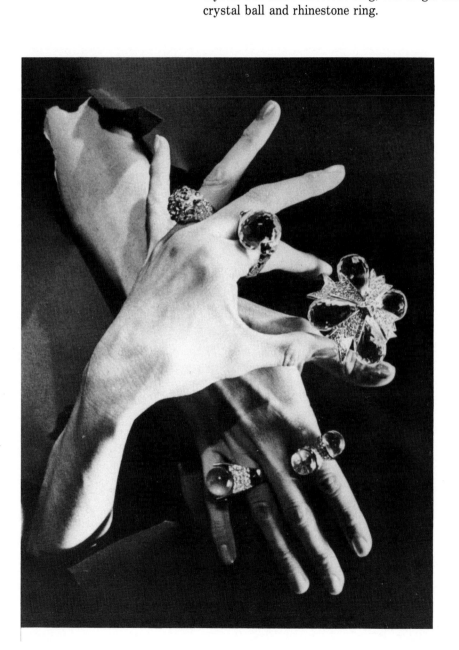

Plate B-20.
Photo Credit: Courtesy Kenneth Jay Lane

Plate B-21 (Below)

Location	Nomenclature	Circa	Description
Full Plate	EARRINGS & NECKLACE	1957	**Hobe'**. Rhinestone collar worn by actress Maureen O'Hara, in **The Wings of Eagles** (MGM, 1957). Metro-Goldwyn-Mayer Studios release, featured **Jewels by Hobe'**.

Plate B-21.
Photo Credit: Courtesy *Jewels by Hobe'*

Plate B-22 (Below)

Location	Nomenclature	Circa	Description
Full Plate	PENDANT-NECKLACE & EARRINGS	1955-65	**Jewels by Hobe'.** Hand-set cultured pearls and genuine gemstones, set in gold-tone metal.

Plate B-22.
Photo Credit: Courtesy *Jewels by Hobe'*

Plate B-23 (Below)

Location	Nomenclature	Circa	Description
Full Plate	Set: CUFF LINKS & TIE-TACK	1935-45	Walrus Tusk Ivory, hand-carved and set with gold nuggets.

Plate B-23.
Author's Collection.
Photo Credit: Dave Hammell

Plate B-24 (Below)

Location	Nomenclature	Circa	Description
Top	CUFF LINKS	1960	Gilded Brass, souvenir "California State Cable R.R. Co." (San Francisco Cable Car).
Center, Left	CUFF LINKS	1960	Souvenir, California State Assembly
Center	TIE BAR, CLIP	1950	Monogram, "DKH", 1/20-12K. Tie bar measures 1¾" x 3/16". (*Dave Hammell Collection*).
Center, Right	CUFF LINKS	1960	The State of Texas souvenir, **Lone Star State**.
Bottom	CUFF LINKS	1960	Souvenir, **American President Lines** (Ocean-going vessels).

Plate B-24.
Allison Dickason Collection unless otherwise noted.
Photo Credit: Dave Hammell

Plate B-25 (Below)

Location	Nomenclature	Circa	Description
Top	CUFF LINKS	1970	**Avon.** Enamelled. Gilded brass. One of a series of antique automobiles.
Center	CUFF STUDS	1950	Mother of Pearl, *fleur-de-lis* design. Modern copy of an Edwardian design. Gilded brass.
Bottom	Set: CUFF LINKS & TIE-TAC w/chain	1960	Die-stamped gold electroplated replica of a 1903 Indian Head penny coin. This type of cut-out coin jewelry was popular in 1930's, then outlawed for **genuine** coinage of U.S.A.

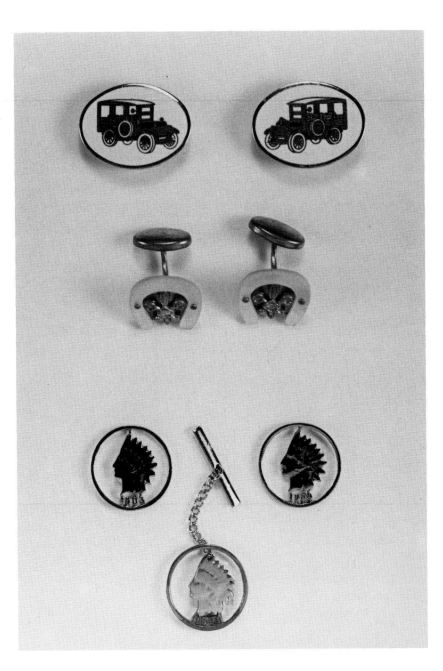

Plate B-25.
Allison Dickason Collection.
Photo Credit: Dave Hammell

Plate B-26 (Below)

Location	Nomenclature	Circa	Description
Top	CUFF LINKS	1960	Exceedingly large pair, antiqued, gold electroplate. (Actual size).
Center	CUFF LINKS	1960	Railroad buff locomotive design. Electroplated.
Bottom	Set: CUFF LINKS & TIE BAR	1965	"Drifty". Logo for Driftwood Dairy, El Monte, California, founded 1930. Available in chrome or goldtone. Sets for men, pendants for women, were LIMITED EDITION Christmas gifts to customers and employees. Manufactured by Brown & Bigelow. Shown actual size.

Plate B-26.
Allison Dickason Collection.
Photo Credit: Dave Hammell

Section III

Unit I
Synopsis of the Years of Fashion Jewelry - (1925-1975)

Unit II
Collections Featured with Plate Numbers

Unit III
Designers and/or Manufacturers Featured with Plate Numbers

Unit IV
Materials Utilized in Jewelry Making

Unit V
Current Manufacturers of Costume Jewelry, Manufacturers of Plastics for The Jewelry Industry, Children's Costume Jewelry, Enamelling Service to Jewelry Manufacturers and Other Suppliers

---

Unit I
Synopsis of the Years of Fashion Jewelry - (1925-1975)

1925-1930 Art Deco Period, with Far East design influence.
Plates: 3, 21, 26, 29, 31, 37, 52 and B-12.

1931-1940 Pre World War II, "Depression-Expression" and Stars of the Silver Screen.
Plates: 3, 13, 16, 21, 22, 26, 29, 32, 36, 37, 38, 40, 52, B-1, B-2, B-3, B-4, B-6, B-7, B-8 and B-9.

1941-1950 The "War Years", post WWII: "Frugal but Flashy". Shortage of metals introduces Art Moderne plastics and composition jewelry -- wild & wily.
Plates: 1, 2, 4, 6, 7, 10, 12, 13, 14, 15, 16, 17, 18, 19, 20, 21, 22, 23, 24, 25, 26, 28, 30, 31, 32, 33, 34, 35, 36, 37, 38, 39, 40, 41, 44, 45, 46, 47, 48, 49, 51, 52, 54, 55, B-1, B-2, B-3, B-4, B-5, B-6 and B-10.

1951-1960 Freedom's Fling -- Acceleration -- Art Moderne advances to ultramodernism.
Plates: 1, 2, 4, 5, 6, 8, 9, 10, 11, 12, 13, 14, 15, 16, 17, 21, 23, 24, 25, 26, 27A, 29, 30, 31, 33, 34, 35, 36, 37, 39, 40, 41, 42, 43, 44, 45, 46, 47, 48, 49, 50, 52, 53, 54, 55, B-2, B-3, B-4, B-5, B-6, B-21 and B-22.

1961-1970 Fancy Free and Flighty -- abstract preoccupation -- "The Flower Children"
Plates: 4, 5, 9, 11, 13, 16, 18, 21, 28, 29, 36, 42, 44, 47, 49, 50, 51, 53, 55, B-3, B-4, B-11, B-13, B-14, B-15, B-16, B-17, B-19, B-20, B-21 and B-22.

1971-1975 Casual -- Cautious -- Crafty
Plates: 4, 51, B-3 and B-18.

Unit II
Collections Featured with Plate Numbers

Lillian Baker (author) 3, 6, 13, 23, 24, 26, 28, 30, 31, 36, 38, 42, 48, 54
Jenny Biddle 30, 34
Bonnie Brown 54
Sharry Clark B-1, B-2, B-3, B-4, B-5, B-6
Mildred Combs 12, 17, 24, 29, 30, 33, 35, 37, 42, 44, 46, 47, 50, 52, 55
Peggy Covey 23, 34
Allison Dickason 9, 12, 17, 22, 24, 27A, 29, 30, 32, 33, 34, 37, 42, 43, 46, 47, 48, 49, 50, 52, 53, 55
Elaine Dill 2, 4, 11, 51
Andrea DiNoto B-11
Susan Ellsworth B-12
Mary Ruth Evry 21, 36, 39, 45
June Forest 23
Nancy Franz B-7, B-8, B-9

G.L. Antiques 13, 16, 25
Barbara L. Hammell 1, 19
Annette Harrelson 48
Mary Harrington 8, 10, 14
Sybel Heller 13, 16, 28
Virginia McCurdy 48
Veronica Newell 32
Fred Silberman B-10
Janet St.Amant 15, 20, 40, 41
Estelle Keevil Tyson 21, 26
Lynn Warech 25, 30, 31, 36
Dr. N.J. Williams 1, 7, 19, 28
Ethel Wilson 5, 6, 18
Jean Wise 39

Photographs of collections, courtesy: Eisenberg Jewelry, Hobe' Cie Ltd. and Kenneth Jay Lane, Inc. [From Company Archives]

Unit III
Designers and/or Manufacturers Featured
with Plate Numbers

Name	Plate Number(s)
ABC Inc.	44
Accessocraft	29, 40
Alice Caviness	53, B-3
Astra	42
Authentic/Vans	40
B.S.K.	42, 47
Beau	46, 52
Boucher	1, 12, 16, 24, 29, 37, 41
Brooks	44
Carnegie, Hattie	21, 29, 50, B-4, B-11
Castlecliff	12, 34, 40, 52
Charel	33
Christian Dior	13, 16, 55
Cini	30, 46
Coro & CoroCraft	13, 17, 23, 24, 42, 54, 55
Coventry	(See Sarah Coventry)
Dali (Elgin American)	40, 41
Dalsheim	42
Danecraft	46, 52
DeMario	24, 45, 53, B-3
DeNicola	23, 41
DiMario	(See DeMario)
Dior	(See Christian Dior)
Eisenberg, Eisenberg Original and Eisenberg Ice	21, 22, 26, 29, 30, 36, 37, 48
Elgin American	40, 41
Emmons	2, 4, 5, 6, 11, 18, 36, 38, 51
Eugene	B-5
Fargo, H.	52
Gerry's	47
Goldette	35
Gray Kingsburg, N.Y.	32
Guillermo Cini	(See Cini)
H. Fargo	52
HAR	17, 29
Haskell	(See Miriam Haskell)
Hattie Carnegie	21, 29, 50, B-4, B-11
Hobe' and Jewels by Hobe'	1, 7, 19, 46, B-21, B-22
Hollycraft	42, 53
J.J.	46, 47
Jeanne	3, 55
Jewelart	46
Jomaz	21, 41, 50
Josef	19
Karu 5th Ave.	47
KJL (Kenneth Jay Lane)	29, B-3, B-13, B-14, B-15, B-16, B-17, B-18, B-19, B-20

Name	Plate Number(s)
Kenneth Jay Lane	(See K.J.L.)
Korda	46
Kramer, and Kramer of N.Y.	25, 30, 34, 36, 37, 40, 49, 50, B-4
Lane	(See K.J.L.)
Ledo	9
Les Bernard, Inc.	45
Manolf	47
Marvella	17, 48
Mazer	13, 16, 23
Mimi	15
Miracle	42
Miriam Haskell	12, 13, 29, 35, 45, 49, B-1, B-2, B-3, B-4, B-5, B-6
Miscellaneous, including patented & copyright (Also see Unmarked)	28, 31, 36, 38
Monet	19, 38, 55
Mosell	17, 26, 35, 44
Napier	15, 20, 34, 40, 45, 53
Nettie Rosenstein	16, 26
Original by Robert	(See Robert)
Panetta	37
Park Lane	47
Pen'n (Pennino)	37
Polcini	47
Regency and Regency Jewels	33, B-3, B-6
Reia	55
Renoir	32, 34
Robert	12, 41, 53, B-2, B-4
Sarah Coventry	8, 10, 14, 42
Schaiparelli	26
Schreiner and Schreiner, N.Y.	28, 47
Standard	37
Stanley Hagler	B-4
Swoboda	17
Symmetalic	24
Theda	46
Tortolani	47
Trifari	9, 16, 26, 28, 29, 33, 36, 37, 38, 39, 42, 43, 48, 50, 55, B-10
Unmarked (also see Miscellaneous)	3, 13, 25, 31, 36, 38
Van Dell	24
Vendome	13, 17, 42, 54
Vogue	B-9
Wiesner	48
Weiss	15, 22, 23, 24, 26, 30, 33, 36, 42, 50, 53, 54

Unit IV
Materials Utilized in Jewelry Making

Ores & Metals		Natural Elements		Man-Made
Aluminum	Iron	Amber	Jade	Bakelite
Brass	Pewter	Bog Oak	Marcasite	Celluloid
Bronze	Palladium	Bone	Pearl	Composition (chemical)
Chrome	Platinum	Coral	Sea Shell	Glass (including "French Jet")
Cinnabar	Rhodium	Coal (Genuine Jet)	Stone (mosaics)	Paste (Brilliants, Strass)
(ore of Mercury)	Silver	Gems & Gemstones	Tortoise-Shell	Plastic Products:
Copper	Steel	Hair	Tooth	"French Ivory", Lucite,
Gold		Horn	Tusk	Resinous and Phenolic by-
		Ivory	Wood	products
				Porcelain

Unit V
Current Manufacturers of Costume Jewelry

A. & J. Jewelry Co., Inc., Providence, RI
Alanco Industries, Inc., New York, NY
Alan Jewelry Co., Providence, RI
Amex Glass & Novelty, Inc., Johnston, RI
Anson, Inc., Providence, RI
Arden Jewelry Mfg. Co., Providence, RI
Beaucraft, Inc., Providence, RI
Carol Jane Creations Co., Inc., Providence, RI
Catamore Co., Inc., E. Providence, RI
Cellini, Inc., Providence, RI
Charles Manufacturing Co., Inc., Providence, RI
Christian Dior--Fashion Jewelry, New York, NY [Marked: "**Christian Dior**"]
Ciner Mfg. Co., Inc., New York, NY [Marked: "**Ciner**" in block letters]
Circle Jewelry Products, Inc., New York, NY
Clementine Jewelry Co., Warwick, RI
Coro, Inc., New York, NY [formerly *Cohn & Rosenenberger, Inc., NY]
Marks:

Americana	**Coro (block)**	**Vanity Fair**
Atomic	**Coro Supreme**	***The Avenue**
Clip-Ease	**Coro-Teens**	***Carraca**
Cocktail Set	**Corograms**	***Eclectra Trisemble**
Constellation	**CoroCraft**	***Coro Radiance**
Coquette	**Jewelcraft**	Adolph Katz, Designer
Coro (script)		

Criterion Consolidated Corp., Woodside, NY
Da Vinci Creations, Inc., Pawtucket, RI
DeLizza & Elster, Inc., Brooklyn, NY
Danal Jewlery Co., Providence, RI
Danecraft, Inc., Providence, RI
Darlene Jewelry Mfg. Co., Pawtucket, RI
Discovery Jewlery Co., Inc., Oakland, CA
Eisenberg Jewelry Co., Chicago, IL [Marked: "**Eisenberg**", "**Eisenberg Ice**" (bold block letters, c.1940), and "**Eisenberg Ice**", script letters, c.1965-current]
Elgin American, Div. of Illinois Watch Case Co., Elgin, IL [Mark: "**Elgin American**"]
Fashion Craft & Jewelry Co., Inc., New York, NY [Mark: "**Original by Robert**"]
Fashion Jewelry Mfg. Co., Inc., Providence, RI
Femic, Inc., Centerdale, RI
Finelli Jewelry, Inc., Providence, RI
Gem-Craft, Inc., Providence, RI
Greenberg, B.B., Co., Providence, RI
Greene Jewelry Mfg. Corp., Providence, RI
Hasco Industries, Inc., New York, NY

Haskell Jewels, Ltd., New York, NY [Marked: "**Miriam Haskell**". Designer, Joseph Hess, c.1930-1965] Current President: Sanford G. Moss, sole owner & stock holder.
Hobe' Jewelry Co., New York, NY [Marked: "**Hobe'**", and "**Jewels by Hobe'**". Designers: Aladdin Cave, Sylvia Hobe, William Hobe]
Hillcraft Co., Johnston, RI
House of Berland, Inc., New York, NY
Jerilou Creations, Inc., Johnston, RI
Jewelry Fashions, Inc., New York, NY
Kenneth Jay Lane, Inc., (Kenneth J. Lane Jewelry Co.), New York, NY [Marks: "**KJL**" and "**Kenneth Jay Lane**". Designer: Kenneth Jay Lane]
Kilnic Co., Providence, RI
Kramer Jewelry Creations, New York, NY [Marks: "**Kramer**", "**Kramer of N.Y.**", "**Original by Kramer**"]
Krementz & Co., Newark, NJ [Mark: "**Kremetz**" and "**Snap-Bar**"/men's jewelry]
Lelaume Mfg. Co., Inc., New York, NY
Lisner-Richlieu Corp., New York, NY
Mercury Industries, Plattsburgh, NY
Monet Div., General Mills Products, Corp., New York, NY [Mark: "**Monet**"]
Originalities of New York, Inc., Woodside, NY
Panetta Jewelry, Inc., New York, NY
Paul Hanson Corp., Jackson, WY
Pell Jewelry Co., Inc., Long Island City, NY
C. Ray Randall Mfg. Co., N. Attleboro, MA
Renoir, Los Angeles, CA [Mark: "**Renoir**" and "**Copperwood**"]
Richton International Corp., New York, NY [AKA Coro]
Ripley & Gowen Co., Providence, RI
Ro-An Jewelry Co., N. Providence, RI
Roth & Steiner, New York, NY
Royal Bead Novelty Co., Inc., New York, NY 10022
Samuel Gold Co., New York, NY
C.H. Stuart & Co., Inc., Newark, NY [Marks: "**Caroline Emmons**", "**Emmons**", "**Sarah Coventry**"]
Syracuse Jewelry Mfg. Co., Syracuse, NY
Tesoro Mfg. Co., Cranston, RI
Trifari, Krussman & Fiskel, Inc., New York, NY (Div. of Hallmark Cards, Inc.) [Mark: "**Trifari**". Designer: Alfred Philippe]
A.M. Wood Co., E. Providence, RI
Wiesner Mfg. Co., Providence, RI
[Note: A comprehensive listing of DESIGNER MARKS, and former manufacturers of COSTUME JEWELRY, including circa dates, can be found in Maryanne Dolan's book, *Collecting Rhinestone Jewelry*, listed in the *Bibliography*.]

Manufacturers of Plastics for the Jewelry Industry

Ace Plastic Co., Inc., Jamaica, NY
Geo. F. Berkander, Inc., Providence, RI
Control Molding Co., Staten Island, NY (Thermo Plastics)
Green Plastics Corp., Hope Valley, RI

Injection Molding Division of Techniplast, Inc., Little Falls, NJ (Molded Plastic)
Magic Novelty Co., Inc., New York, NY
Melmar Plastics, Inc., New York, NY
Polyform Plastics Corp., New York, NY

Children's Costume Jewelry
Uncas Mfg. Co., Providence, RI

Enamelling Service to Jewelry Manufacturers

Goldman Kolber, Inc., New York, NY
SYNTHETICS - Moster Jewel Co., Perth Amboy, NJ

COLLECTIBLE SOUVENIR - Fort, Inc., E. Providence, RI
METAL FINDINGS - Magic Novelty Co., Inc., New York, NY

Other Suppliers

Aetna Jewelry Mfg. Co., Providence, RI [Rhinestone Jewelry]
E.A. Baleau Company, Providence, RI
Celart Jewelry Co., Inc., Providence, RI [Sterling/Gold Filled/Electroplate/Brass]
Marvel Jewelry Mfg. Co., Cranston, RI [Sterling]

B. David Co., Cincinnati, OH [Rhinestones/Gold filled/Sterling]
International Gem Corp., Levittown, NY [Cut Gemstones]
Mey Co., East Orange, NJ [Imitation Stones & Rhinestones]
Wiesner Mfg. Co., Providence, RI [Electroplate]

Section IV

Alphabetical Cross-Reference Index
by Subject or Nomenclature, with Plate Numbers

Subject or Nomenclature   **Plate Numbers**

American Indian Design B-7

Animals (various species) 1, 6, 9, 11, 29, 46, 47, 50, 51, B-10

Antique, heirloom reproductions influenced by Oriental, Egyptian, Etruscan, Indian, Georgian and Victorian design 1, 3, 4, 7, 11, 17, 19, 20, 30, 31, 32, 35, 39, 44, 46, 49, 51, B-2, B-5, B-6, B-16

Art Deco design 3, 21, 37, D-5

Art Moderne (Also see "Pop Art") 4, 8, 10, 11, 15, 27, 28, 32, 34, 35, 38, 51, 54, 55

Aurora Borealis beads and sets 11, 13, 18, 25, 30, 33, 34, 42, 53, 54, B-3, B-6

Bakelite . . . . (See Plastic)

Beads (Also see Necklaces) 3, 13, 23, 24, 31, 43, 53, 54, B-2, B-3, B-4, B-5, B-14

Belt 20

Belt Buckle 52

Billiken (also spelled Billikin) B-23

Birds 9, 17, 27, 38, 40, 41, 44, 46, 47, 55

Bow (or Ribbon design) 15, 24, 40, B-9

Bracelets 3, 4, 14, 15, 16, 21, 22, 30, 32, 33, 36, 39, 41, 44, 45, 46, 51, 52, 54, B-4, B-12, B-13

Brooch . . . . (See Pins)

Butterflies 25, 30, 33, 37

Cameos 3, 7, B-5

Chains 4, 8, 19, 20, 27, 28

Choker . . . . 52, B-1, B-8(a), B-14, B-15

Christmas Tree 42, 53

Chrome (Also see Rhodium) B-11

Crystal . . . . (See Rhinestone)

Collar (Also see Choker) 15, 25, B-21

Comb B-6

Compact 40, 41

Copper 32, 34

Cross (including varied designs) 2, 4, 11, 40, B-20

Crown Design 2, 13, 29, 47

Cuff Links B-23, B-24, B-25, B-26

"Dog Collar" . . . . (See Choker)

Dress Clip 21, 36

Earrings 1, 5, 7, 13, 16, 17, 21, 26, 28, 29, 30, 32, 33, 34, 35, 36, 37, 38, 39, 40, 42, 44, 50, 52, 53, 55, B-1, B-3, B-5, B-7, B-14, B-15, B-17, B-18, B-19, B-21

Egyptian Design 3, 32, 35, 50

Enamel 4, 9, 11, 17, 24, 26, 31, 32, 39, 41, 42, 43, 44, 51

Fans 6, 17

Figurals 1, 4, 9, 11, 17, 23, 24, 25, 29, 30, 33, 37, 38, 40, 41, 42, 44, 46, 47, 50, 51, 55, B-10

Fish 24, B-11

Flowers (including botannical motifs) 4, 6, 8, 9, 12, 13, 14, 16, 24, 26, 35, 36, 38, 39, 40, 41, 42, 43, 45, 48, 52, 55

Fur Clips 13, 26, 29, 37, 55

Gemstones (genuine) 1, 7, 17, 19, 26, B-22

Goldtone (including Gold-tone, and electroplate) . . 1, 2, 6, 9, 12, 13, 14, 16, 17, 20, 24, 26, 28, 29, 31, 33, 34, 39, 40, 41, 42, 43, 44, 45, 47, 49, 50, 51, 54, 55, B-2, B-14, B-16, B-19, B-20, B-22

Hair Barrett 14

Hair Ornament B-6

Hat Ornaments D-1, D-3, D-4, D-6

Hatpins D-2, D-5

Heart Motifs 7, 19, 20, 26, 46

Insects 3, 9

Jade (genuine and simulated) 14, 17, 26, B-18

Kilt Pin 42

Locket 7

Lucite . . . . (See Plastic)

Medallion 4

Metals (antiqued, oxidized, burnished or japanned) . . 1, 6, 7, 11, 19, 20, 21, 23, 27, 32, 35, 45, 46, 51, 55, B-1, B-4, B-5, B-7, B-16

Mythological & Symbolic (Also see Cross) 3, 23, 30, 35, 44, 46, 50, 55, B-7

Necklace (Also see Beads, Pendants, Chokers, and Collars) 1, 12, 19, 22, 27, 28, 31, 32, 34, 35, 37, 38, 39, 44, 52, 53, B-1, B-2, B-5, B-7, B-16, B-17, B-18, B-19, B-21

Oriental design 1, 9, 14, 17, 26, B-18

Parure (3 or more pieces and Sets of 2 matching pieces) 2, 4, 5, 6, 7, 8, 10, 11, 12, 15, 16, 17, 18, 19, 20, 22, 23, 25, 26, 31, 33, 34, 36, 41, 43, 44, 48, 49, 50, 54, B-1, B-3, B-5, B-7, B-15, B-17, B-18, B-19, B-21, B-22

Pearls (imitation, cultured, oriental) 2, 5, 6, 9, 12, 14, 18, 40, 45, 47, 48, 49, 50, 51, B-1, B-2, B-3, B-4, B-17, B-22

Pendants (Also see Necklaces) 3, 19, 28, 31, 37, 46, B-7, B-11, B-16, B-19, B-22

Pins and Brooches. (Also see Kilt Pin, Scarf Pin & "Scatter" Pin) . . . 1, 2, 3, 6, 7, 9, 11, 12, 13, 14, 15, 16, 17, 18, 19, 23, 24, 25, 26, 28, 29, 30, 33, 34, 35, 36, 37, 38, 39, 40, 41, 42, 43, 44, 45, 46, 47, 48, 49, 50, 51, 52, 53, 54, 55, B-1, B-2, B-3, B-4, B-6, B-9, B-10, B-20

Plastic (Bakelite, Celluloid, resin, lucite, "French Ivory", & other composition plastics) 3, 4, 38, 43, 50, B-10, B-11, B-12, D-5

"Pop Art" B-11

Religious Symbols 1, 2, 4, 11, B-20

Resin . . . . (See Plastic)

Rhinestone (including crystal) . . . . . 5, 8, 15, 16, 21, 22, 36, 37, 39, 48, B-1, B-2, B-3, B-4, B-8 (a) & (b), B-9, B-14, B-15, B-16, B-17, B-18, B-19, B-20, B-21

Rhodium (Also see Chrome) . . . . . 4, 5, 8, 10, 15, 18, 21, 22, 23, 25, 36, 37, 38, 48, B-8 (a) & (b)

Ring 8, 18, B-5, B-13, B-20

Scarf Pin 29, 37, 38, 49, 52, B-4

"Scatter" Pin 9, 11, 23, 28, 44, 46, 47, 51

Sets . . . . (See *Parure*)

Sterling (Also see *Vermeil*) 23, 26, 30, 37, 38, 46, 52, B-10

Symbolic (Religious, Mythological, Commemorative, Insignia & Zodiac) 3, 4, 6, 9, 23, 29, 30, 35, 36, 46, 50, 55, B-20

Tie Bar and Tie Tac B-23, B-24, B-25, B-26

Turquoise (genuine and immitation) . . . 1, 4, 13, 23, 31, 41, 43, 44, 50, B-7

Vermeil (gold karat or gold wash over sterling silver) 16, 21, 24, 29, 55, B-9

Wood 38

Zodiac (Also see Symbolic) 30

Section V

Glossary of Jewelry Items

Pronunciation of Foreign Terms and Types

ABALONE - ăb-ă-lō'-nĕ

Sea-shell creature of the Pacific Coast with an inner-shell lining of gray/pink natural pearlized substance. Used extensively by Indian Tribes of the West. The beautiful lustre inspired its further utilization in combination with silver and beads during the early forties and again cunningly incorporated in fashion jewelry of the seventies and eighties.

ACCESSORIES

Jeweled accessories held a prominent place in late 19th and 20th Century high fashion, especially as introduced by Coco Chanel in the 1920's, and into the 1930's. Accessories were utilitarian but combined utility with beauty of design. The *lorgnette*, buckles, short hatpins and hat ornaments, dress clips, sash pins, beaded bags and purses were very popular, and the "necessaries" included: coin purses, vanity cases, card cases and tiny writing tablets complete with silver case and lead pencil. These accessories added an expression of charm to the individual costume. The Art Deco period, c. 1925, brought the powder and rouge compact, with bright lipsticks, and even the elongated cigarette holder which gave a contrived saucy stance to the faddish fashion models of the era.

AGATE

A variety of quartz or natural gemstone, the most common being the banded or striped agate. Among the varieties of quartz known as agate, is black onyx often used for cameos and *intaglios*. The carnelian or red agate from Scotland was very popular for kilt pins and brooches, while Brazilian agate and those mined in India contributed to requirements for the mass-produced jewelry in the late 19th and 20th centuries. Several designers combined agate gemstones in various colors with crystal and rhinestones heightened by colored foil, in the high fashion jewelry known as "costume jewelry".

AIGRETTE - ă' grĕt

A hair ornament consisting of a plume or spray of glitter, often accentuated by either a jewel or buckle. Worn in the hair, or attached to a head-band, *aigrettes* were still being worn through the twenties and early 1930's.

AMBER

A yellowish-brown fossil resin. Also found in black and varieties of brown and orange. Amber comes from ancient forests of fir trees, or mined from under the Baltic Sea. Orange color amber comes from Sicily. Recent amber has been fashioned into jewelry by designers utilizing Scandanavian amber.

AMETHYST

A gemstone found in shades from pale lavender to deep purple. A crystalized quartz found in Russia, Brazil, Uruguay, Ceylon and the United States. The color purple denotes the color of royalty. Amethyst stones were often worn as a "cure for drunkeness".

ANTIMONY

The mineral, stibnite, used to impart hardness in alloys. Antimony is now another word for a tin-white colored metal used extensively in costume jewelry castings. It expands as it solidifies, and becomes brittle. Antimony is a "pot metal" base for rhodium plating or other types of gilding.

ARABESQUE - ăr' ab-ĕsk

Flowing scrollwork, often in low relief, epitomized by curlicues of line.

ART DECO (1910-1930)

A stilted, stylized design which was named after the 1925 *L'Exposition Internationale des Arts Decoratifs et Industriels Modernes*, held in Paris, France. Much of the Art Deco design was a transition from the earlier *Art Nouveau*, and as with the *nouveau* epoch, was inspired by the art of the American Indian, ancient Egyptian and Greek and Roman architecture. The early 1920's interest in Cubism and Dadism as a new art form, greatly influenced the Art Deco period. The King Tut travelling exhibit, in the 1970's, renewed the craze for Egyptian design jewelry. Additionally, the mysteries of the Pyramids and a continuing revival of astrological studies, lent itself to Art Deco designs which in turn were incorporated in the Art Moderne period following 1930.

ART MODERNE (1935-1945)

It is generally accepted that the period of the 1920's to the 1930's is the Art Deco period. The decade of the 1940-1950 is considered the "modern" period, an era in which just about any conceivable type of design -- whether it be flamboyant or contrived with delicate fancy -- survived. However, the Art Moderne period (1935-1945) avoided such frivolous swirls and instead "streamlined" into crisp geometric lines, all designs of decorative and utilitarian art forms. "Modern" seems to be a term giving license to all creativity in any form, be it eccentric or strictly along conventional jeweler's line. The Art Moderne period expresses the conflict between machine and nature which is so evident in Art Deco. But Art Moderne contains somewhat less contrived artistry, although some pieces do appear as near absurdities. Most Art Moderne jewelry combines phenolics and modern metals such as chrome and rhodium. However, there has been great jewelry pieces executed in 3-dimensional Art Moderne form, designed by the famed artists, George Braque and Salvador Dali.

ART NOUVEAU - art nū-vō

Refer to Lillian Baker's book, *Art Nouveau & Art Deco Jewelry*, published by COLLECTOR BOOKS, Paducah, Kentucky, 1981. This is the first book entirely devoted to these two periods which produced some of the most collectible jewelry sought after in the 1980's. A note from the author states, "A simplistic but hearty definition of *Art Nouveau* and Art Deco design is the triumph over functional line by artistic merit." Its full meaning is in the text.

ALLOY

Combination of metals fused together. A base metal mixed with a precious ore to make it workable, to harden it, or to change its color.

BAGS (See PURSES)

BAGUETTE - bă-gĕt′

A narrow rectangular-cut stone most often chosen for diamonds. A **baquette**-cut was influenced by the interest in Cubism of the 1920's. When associated with emeralds, it is called an "emerald-cut".

BAKELITE (Also see PLASTICS)

A trademark for a synthetic resin chemically formulated and named after Belgian chemist, L.H. Backeland (1909). This newer plastic was for molding items formerly created in the highly flammable Celluloid or in hard rubber molds. It is capable of being molded and carved, and some *art nouveau* and deco jewelry pieces were crafted in Bakelite.

BAROQUE - bă-rŏk′

Bold, ornate, heavy-looking ornamentation.

BARRETT

Another name for barrett is "hair clasp", particularly those into which a beautiful silk or grosgrain ribbon bow could be inserted. Barrettts are available in elegant gold or silver plate, highly chased and engraved, and some were also offered in sterling and gold karat. Metallic barretts were marketed through the 1920's and from the twenties to the present time. Many handsome barretts are made of various plastics, including those set with rhinestones, gems and gemstones. Sterling barretts were more popular after the 1930's.

BASSE-TAILLE - bass-ā-tiĕ

A type of enamelling in which a metal plate is cut to various depths into which translucent enamel is poured, thus achieving a 3-dimensional effect. The depth of relief produces shadings from light to dark. The deeper the metal is incised, the darker the color; where shallow routing occurs, the shading is almost transparent. This routing is worked *intaglio*, the opposite of *repousse* work. (See *INTAGLIO* and *REPOUSSE*).

BEAD

An ornament of varied shapes and sizes, with a hole end to end into which a needle can be inserted for stringing or mounting. Most glass beads came from Czechoslovakian, Italian and American glass-blowing factories. However, René Lalique is known to have made and sold beads through his catalogue and shop. Beads are made from gemstones, metals, shells, seeds, ivory, bone, stone, horn and *paper-maché*. Glass beads are made on a blowing rod and then pierced for stringing on thread, wire and many natural and man-made fibres.

BEZEL

A groove or flange which holds a stone secure in its setting.

BELTS

Metallic discs and chains were worn to accentuate a small waist. The chasing and engraving on the metal was executed to pick up the pattern of the lace on the garment being worn, or to complement the fashionable design of the frock. Buckles often were designed with art deco motifs, combining plastics with metals.

BIJOUTERIE - bĕ-z′hŏo t-rĕ

Jewelers working in media of metals, usually gold and silver, as opposed to those in the gem-setting industry. Metals were worked to produce elegant pieces and "trinkets of virtue".

BILLIKEN (or Billikin)

An original good luck charm conceived and patented in 1908 by Florence Pretz, from Kansas City, Missouri. The Craftsman's Guild, and The Billiken Company (Chicago), were the principle manufacturers of this novelty.

The original American design was first copied by the Eskimos in walrus tusk ivory and whale's teeth. From 1925 through 1965, copies were manufactured in Germany, Czechoslavakia, and Japan. These were fabricated in glass, porcelain, metals and other media.

According to researcher/collector, Dorothy Jean Ray, the artist/designer Florence Pretz was influenced by Asian figures such as Buddha or Taoist gods. Another influence was Palmer Cox's pixie-like "Brownies". It is interesting to note that according to Ms. Ray, "Kewpies" came **after** Billikens.

Dorothy Jean Ray's article, "THE BILLIKEN", is available from Alaska Northwest Publishing Co., 130 Second Ave. South, Edmonds, WA 98020. This fine work appeared in *The Alaska History and Arts of the North Quarterly Journal*, Winter 1974, Vol. 4, No. 1. It contains fascinating history, photographs and excellent references. A must for Billiken buffs.

BIRTHSTONE JEWELRY (see GEMS)

BLACK GLASS JEWELRY (Also see JET)

Imitation jet or onyx.

BLISTER PEARL

Irregularly shaped pearly deposit in oyster which is sometimes hollow, as opposed to a *baroque* pearl which is a **solid** irregular shaped pearl.

BOG OAK

A dark brown peat-like material used especially by the Irish for inexpensive jewelry. It is a carved material and is not molded like black glass or "French Jet".

BOX SETTING

A stone enclosed in a box-shaped setting with edges of metal pressed down to hold it in place. Sometimes referred to as a "Gypsy" mounting.

BRACELETS

Bracelets have been popular since time immemorial. Art Deco artisans produced "jointed" wide-cuffed bracelets and unjointed bangle-type bracelets, the latter often given in friendship. Adjustable bracelets were worn by both ladies and infants and had an adjustable "expando" mechanism. Because Queen Victoria's Prince Consort presented her with a wedding ring in the form of a pair of entwined serpents, bracelets with this motif were very much in vogue during her long reign. With the discovery of King Tut's tomb, the serpent again became a symbol in many pieces of jewelry, and most eloquently in the bracelets of the *Nouveau*, Deco, and Moderne eras. The bangle bracelet was originally called a "bangle ring", although it was made to fit around the wrist. It resembled an enlarged ring and was called "bangle ring" because the wire was very narrow and resembled a wedding band. The adjustable cuff or band bracelet was another innovation of the 1890's, as was the coil or mesh wire bracelet. Coil bracelets were adjustable in that being a coil the bracelet could be stretched to fit. The "wedding band" type of bracelet could also be expanded with either end separating and then popping together after it was placed on the wrist. As late as 1910, the stiff band or cuff bracelet was still preferred and measured from 1" to 2" wide. High relief and much *niello* work (black tracery enamel) were featured on cuff bracelets, especially those imported from the Orient. Catalin or Marblette plastic bracelets of the deco and moderne periods gained enormous popularity during those periods (1925-1945) followed by the enormous appeal of flexible wrist ornaments of rhodium studded with rhinestones and imitation gemstones of foiled crystal to dazzle the fashion world. Bracelets became so fashionable that they were worn in varied quantities and designs, sometimes at the wrist or as arm-bands -- like some colorful tattoo. The wristwatch band of the 1960's and 1970's became bracelets with hidden timepieces, thus a piece of jewelry which was not only decorative but functional as well.

BRASS

A yellowish-gold color metal which is primarily an alloy of copper, tin, zinc or other base metal. Brass is the base for much gilded or gold-washed jewelry of the deco period.

BRILLIANTS

Another term for paste, *strass*, crystal or rhinestones.

BRIOLETTE - brē' ŏ-lĕt'

An oval or pear-shaped diamond entirely faceted in triangular cuts. Most popular after platinum mountings were introduced in early 20th century and modern jewelry.

BROOCH (see PINS)

BUCKLES

Buckles were wrought for belts, cummerbunds, sashes, shoes, capes and hats. Some belt buckles were actually brooch-pins with simulated hasps. The buckle was pinned in front of a sash, belt, cummerbund or hat. Buckles were finished in Roman gold, rose gold, antique gold, silver, French grey, oxidized metals, gun metal and were made of the plastics and chrome of the deco and moderne periods. They were most fashionable after the turn-of-the-century. When the belt buckle was designed to meet at an angle, rather than in a horizontal manner, it was called the "new dip" belt buckle. Shirtwaists were "in" at this same period and women demanded buckles that matched pins and studs, as well as hatpins and collar stays. Colonial-type shoe buckles came in oxidized silver and were used to accent a brown or black calfskin pump with a very high tongue. The clasp of the tongue fit into the colonial buckle, and the shoe was called "Colonial Pump" because this type buckle was a reproduction of the earlier fashion. Many colonial-type shoe buckles were of beautiful cut steel. The color of the metal was known as "French Gray", and the steel was often hand etched within its square shape. Soon these types gave way to many new shapes, particularly the oblong. In the 1915-1925 era, there arrived a new color, "brown jewelry", which was a kind of seal-brown tone of metal which went very well with the popular brown fabric coming into vogue at the beginning of the 20th Century. In the second decade of the 20th Century, the sash buckle with the simulted hasp was introduced on wider cummerbund-type belts which were worn closer to the hips rather than to the waist, a fashion note of the deco period. Small waists were "in" until after World War I, when the flapper girl costume brought the so-called "waistline" to well below the

curve of the hip -- a fashion revived today. Since the 1970's, belts of fabric and leather have been shown with detachable buckles which are made in various shapes, metallic content, and fine cloisonne enamelling.

BUTTONS (Dress)

Some dress buttons came in sets of three and were joined by a very delicate lovely link chain which prevented loss. The stud end was worn inside the blouse which, prior to 1900, was called a "waist". From 1900 to 1920, the waist was then called a "shirt", even for women. During the deco period, it became a "blouse", and has remained thus to the present day. Buttons were beautifully engraved, enamelled, with raised borders, and some were set with garnets, pearls or turquoise. Identical buttons in miniature were made for children's wear, although often simpler in design. Buttons not only came in the round, but were bar shape, oblong shape and oval shape. During the deco and moderne periods, buttons had beautifully curved designs, wonderfully engraved with lovely rippled or ribbed cable patterns. These were made of both natural and man-made materials -- and especially glass. Most metallic buttons were die-stamped, but others were handcrafted. The deco and moderne plastic buttons were often enhanced by foiled rhinestones of many colors, sizes and shapes. New machine manufacture and plastic compositions which lends itself to injection molding, produced extraordinary designs, shapes and colors. With modern methods of fastenings and invisible closures made possible by modern space technology thermal plastics, buttons are now more decorative rather than functional, and in many cases have become obsolete.

CABACHON - kȧ-bo̊-shôn'

A stone without facets, and shaped like a dome.

CAGE (See MOUNTINGS)

CAIRNGORM - kȧm'-gorm'

A yellow or smoky brown clear quartz, mined especially in Cairngorm, Scotland and featured in Scottish brooches and jeweled accessories.

CAMEO

Conch shell, onyx gem, coral and various gemstones which were carved in either relief or *intaglio*. Cameos are also molded in synthetics such as plastic or glass. Cameos usually depict a scene or portrait, but may be symbolic. Ivory and wood can also be carved into a cameo, but **natural** elements **cannot be molded.**

CAMEO *HABILLE* - ăh-bē̄-ă'

Usually a portrait cameo in which the male or female model has been enhanced by the addition of a diamond or other gem imbedded as a brooch, necklace, hat ornament or even a ring. Sometimes small diamonds or pearls may be added simply as an accent or for enhancement.

CARAT (English/European) or KARAT (American)

Standard unit of weight for gems and gemstones, or a measure for gold tabled at 1/24th part of pure gold in an alloy, i.e. 14K or carat: 14 parts gold, 10 parts alloy.

Marks on gold began about 1890. European and English gold marks were in **carats**, (9 ct., 15 ct. or 18ct.). American jewelry was primarily 14K (karat), but America and Canada also made 12K and 18K gold jewelry. (One carat is approximately 4 grains.)

Early Victorian pieces were made before the stringent hallmarking of gold was in effect, and 10 carat gold was used for less expensive pieces.

The term "CARAT" is a symbol for the unit weight of precious gems. It is also used in establishing the weight of gemstones. In diamonds, it's 200 milligrams per one carat, setting the weight standard for other precious gems.

Pearls are also measured by carat grains. The international acceptance of 200 milligrams per carat occurred in 1916 in Great Britain, France, Holland and the United States -- all industrial centers for trade in gold and gems.

CARBUNCLE

A garnet gem that has been cabachon-cut.

CARNELIAN (also spelled CORNELIAN)

A variety of chalcedony with a wax-like luster. An ornamental stone found mainly in Greece or in Asia Minor. Carnelian has a translucent color which may be deep red, flesh red or reddish-white. It takes a good polish and cut, and is ideal for seals and *intaglios*.

CARNIVAL GLASS

Specifically iridescent glass made in America from 1910-1930. Usually in pressed patterns, it was mostly manufactured by Northwood Glass Co., (Ohio); Imperial Glass Company, (Ohio); and The Fenton Art Glass Company, (West Virginia). Carnival glass was utilized as ornamental heads for hatpins, circa 1930-1940. There were thousands of various patterns produced, and these mold patterns are found in buttons made in the same period.

CARTOUCHE´ - kăr-tooͦsh´

A shield or scroll with curved edges used pariculary on gold or silver for a monogram. A *cartouché* should not be confused with an *escutcheon*. An escutcheon is a plate of metal added or applied to the top of a signet or monogram type hatpin head, or to any other piece of jewelry such as a ring or brooch.

CASTING

To form a plastic or liquid substance into a particular shape so as to **form** the shape (most often in metal). The heated metal is poured and then allowed to harden and take shape in the mold.

Casting usually is associated with metallic work, whereas molding is more descriptive of an injection type of process such as for plastic or for molding glass. One can also mold a pliable material into a particular shape, such as clay, plaster-of-Paris, rubber, etc., so these molds can be used for castings or reproduction work.

A mold is a cavity into which anything is shaped, thus regulating the size, form, pattern, or design of an object. (See TEMPLET and PROTOTYPE).

CELLULOID (also see BAKELITE & PLASTICS)

A trademark of Hyatt Bros., Newark, NJ (1868). It is a composition mainly of soluble guncotton and camphor, resembling ivory in texture and color. Celluloid was also dyed to imitate coral, tortoise-shell, amber, malachite, etc. Originally called **xylonite**, Celluloid is the word most often used to describe any imitation ivory, bone or tortoise. But there were many other imitators of such natural elements: "ivorine", "French ivory", "tortine" and the like. Celluloid should not be confused with the harder and more resiliant plastic known as Bakelite, Catalin or Marblette. Celluloid, being highly flammable, lost favor to phenolic resins of the 1930's. Celluloid was first used as synthetic ivory in the manufacture of billiard balls.

CELTIC DESIGN

Primarily junctured lines and discs affiliated with the ancient Celtic Cross. The designs are derived from Gaulic, British, Irish, Scotch and Welsh symbols and have been incorporated in much modern design revived in the 1930's.

CHAINS

Probably the most widely used chain is the ordinary neck chain with a clasp to attach a pendant, watch, locket, medallion, etc. When Queen Victoria married Prince Albert in 1849, immediately there was a chain named for him--the "Albert Chain"--consisting of a lapel bar on one end and swivel or tongue-pin on the other. It was worn draped across the vest. At the center of this chain was a little jump ring for a small fob-type medallion or charm. A woman's chain of the same period was similar to the Albert Chain but much shorter and was called the "Victoria" or "Queen Chain". It usually had several charms dangling from various interruptions in the linkage. Vest chains were made mostly in solid gold, or in either 10K or 14K with a great variety of linkages. There were square, oval, flat, square twist and ship's cable, among many others. The vest chain was also popularized by the visit of Charles Dickens to America, and eventually showed up in 1893 catalogues under "Dickens Vest Chain". Men wore their vest chains slung across the front of their vests, and women's "vest chains" were smaller duplicates of the men's chains except that they were more intricately and more delicately wrought than a man's. The woman's vest chains differed in that they had slides which shortened or tightened the chain which was then draped into a belt or pinned to the waist-shirt.

The slides on women's neck chains had many variations in design, and often exhibited intricate patterns studded with genuine gems and decorative gemstones. By adjusting the slide, the chain was prevented from encircling either side of a woman's bosom, centering the chain at the point of cleavage. Neck chains for women could average as long as 48", but always included that necessary slide which would keep the chain from slipping off the shoulder or looping a breast.

There were many neck chains, some in 10K or 14K gold. The usual length of a neck chain was from 12" to 13½". Manufactured in various lengths today, they come in twisted wire, woven wire, plain link chains, barrel links, chased wire and flat links. These neck chains, or "necklaces" as they are sometimes called, still accomodate small charms, lockets or pendants. The links on the chains vary from square, round and octagon shape, all with chased wire or extremely fancy linkage. In the 1970's, men's vest chains and hip chains for watches, came back into vogue to accomodate the nostaglic bent toward pocket watches. Multiple chains in graduated and varied sizes were all the rage for young girls and women in the 1960's, on into the early 1980's.

CHALCEDONY - kăl-sĕd´-o·ni

An ornamental stone found in Asia Minor, primarily Greece, which has a translucent quality. It is a variety of quartz. The term chalcedony denotes a grayish or milky-colored quartz including the family of onyx, agate, sard, cat's eye, jasper, carnelian and chrysoprase. All take high polish and are suitable for good *intaglio* work except for the cat's eye which is polished into a cabochon-cut stone.

CHAMPLEVE - shămp´ lĕ-vǎ (also see ENAMELLING)

An enamelling technique in which areas of metal are cut, etched or routed and filled with enamel. Unlike *cloisonne*, the cells are cut rather than formed by wires, (*cloisons*). *Champleve* is most commonly applied to copper or bronze. The metals are gilded on exposed and visible surfaces.

CHANNEL SETTING

A series of stones set close together in a straight line with the sides of the mounting gripping the outer edges of the stones.

CHARMS

Most recently, costume jewelry charms are of low carat or gold plate. Many are set with assorted colored stones, not necessarily genuine gems. Very often, charms are designed as lockets. Some can open; other have fronts that can slide out to reveal a photo of a loved one. Many charms are of sterling, German silver or silver-plate. Occasionally, one will find charms in rhodium. Charms are in many instances considered "love tokens", which include Christian symbols, hearts, animals, fish, fruit, clocks, insects, compasses, signets, novelties, mechanical devices, carpenter's tools, firearms, vehicles, lanterns, shoes, fraternal charms--anything that imagination could allow--were makings of Charms.

CHASING

The ornamentation of metal with grooves or lines with the use of hand-chisels and hammers. Obverse (front) chasing is called *intaglio*; chasing from the reverse side, (back) is called *repousse*.

CHATELAINE - shăt'-e-lăn

A decorative clasp or a hook from which many chains are hung to accomodate various household accessories such as thimbles, scissors, keys, files or to display jeweler's conceits such as watches, seals and other decorative implements. From *chatelaines* hung various "necessaries", such as a miniature fan, glove buttoner, or a dog whistle. There were also grooming devices: an ear spoon for cleaning the ears, a sharp pick for cleaning under the nails, as well as a toothpick.

Very short *chatelaine* chains were called *chatelettes*. They measured from 2″ to 6″ in length. An ornamental pin or brooch was attached, although the jewelry could be worn separately. The *chatelette* chain had a swivel at the end of the chain from which to hang a watch. The brooch was in the popular bowknot or pansy wrought in *baroque* fashion or an unusual twisted design. Early *chatelaines* were worn at the waist, but in more recent times, the clasp-type was pinned to the dress or waist, then caught up at the end of the chain and pinned again by another ornament. Silver card cases, coin holders and vanity cases comprised the *chatelaines* of the 1925-1940 years, when the *chatelaine* ring was introduced. From the tiny, short chain, came a clasp which secured a handkerchief, and vanity cases equipped to hold scent pills, a little mirror, straight pins, coins, a lipstick and powder puff. The introduction of rhinestone studded plastic evening purses during the deco period ended the long-reigning *chatelaine*. Over-sized bags and purses became recipients of "modern" women's "necessaries", including cosmetic cases, wallets, address books and other toiletries too numerous to mention.

CHINOISERIE - shĕ nwă'/z'-rĕ

Decoration or ornamentation "in the Chinese manner".

CHOKER

A single-strand necklace or ribbon which fits snugly around the throat. The single strand could be made of pearls, gems or beads, but could also consist of several strands of metallic chain accentuated by a central brooch. The ribbon-type choker was made of *grosgrain* or velvet. To this ribbon was added a brooch, either center or off-center, determined by the particular taste of the wearer. In the early 1950's, a new type of choker was introduced as a "dog collar". These were much more elaborate and consisted of solid castings of metal blazing with rhinestones of intricate cut and set into lavish designs. The "dog collar" embraced the throat sometimes as high up as under the chin and down to the shoulders. Combinations of rhinestones and pearls or varied chains studded or spaced with rhinestone sets, cascaded in row upon row from the throat, narrowing into large pendants which dangled upon the chest or bosom. Some of the most extraordinary examples came in the 1970's, followed by a renewed interest in feminine evening attire of the 1980's.

CHROME (also called Chromium)

The word comes from the Greek "chroma", which means color. Chrome is a metal that forms very hard steel-gray masses that gleam a silver color. Less than 3% mixture of chromium to steel produces an extremely hard alloy. It is used for plating base metals that easily corrode. It receives its name from the green, orange, yellow, red, etc., colors which emanate from the oxide and acid which contacts specific minerals and yields a chrome-green, chrome-yellow and other color pigments. Chrome-plated jewelry is not common since it was an experimental metal proving to be more expensive than silver-color platings of nickle and pewter. One may occasionally come upon a chrome and plastic brooch or bracelet from the Art Deco or Art Moderne Periods. These pieces are highly collectible not only because of scarcity, but because the combination and designs of the periods lent uniqueness to each and every piece.

CHRYSOPRASE - krĭs'-ŏ-prăz

Apple-green in color, it is actually a dyed chalcedony or agate which has a cloud-like rather than a brilliant color. It is almost like "vasoline" glass, seemingly with an oily surface. This stone was very popular during the Art Deco and Art Moderne periods, particularly when combined with marcasites and silver.

CINNABAR

Cinnabar is the only important ore of Mercury and is a brilliant red or vermillion color mineral used as a red pigment. Most popular in China, the origin of the word is probably Chinese. The color is sometimes referred to as "dragon's blood". The pigment is highly prized by Chinese artisans for dying inlay work for jewelry and other artifacts. Cinnabar is a term often misused when referred to as a "gemstone".

CITRINE

A pale lemon-colored gemstone of the quartz variety often mistaken for topaz.

CLASPS

The "push-in" type clasp is the oldest form of clasp on a bracelet or necklace. Brooch clasps had simple hooks under which a pin-shank was held in place. Eventually, safety-type devices were added. The "ball-catch" safety type of clasp consists of a ¾ circle with a small lever-type tab which completes the round, securely locking the brooch-pin. This "ball-catch" was innovated in 1911 and helps date pins and brooches.

A "spring-ring" clasp is in the shape of a tiny circle with a push-pin on a spring which opens and springs shut for closure of a necklace or bracelet. This is the most common type of clasp device and is found on most modern jewelry made after the turn-of-the-century.

Ornamental clasps were worn until the 1930's, when there came the simple screw-barrel type usually found on beads. This was followed by a chain with an open "fish-hook" type of appliance which could hook into the linkage of the chain, thus making it adjustable to the size of the wearer.

Prior to die-stamped jewelry and again in the 1930's, clasps were usually incorporated in the overall design of necklaces, pendants, chains, chokers and bracelets. All finer designed, more expensive pieces, had such clasps, including high fashion jewelry from 1925-1975. Some designers fashioned fabulous clasps to be worn either at the back or as an ornament to be shown at the side of the neck or directly in front to further enhance the wearer.

New types of safety clasps, with and without safety chains, have entered the jewelry trade, but these are usually found on expensive gold and gemstone jewelry.

CLAW-SET (Sometimes called "Tiffany-set")

Tiny claws or prongs which are curved to hold down a stone in its setting.

CLIPS (Dress Clips, Fur Clips & Sweater Clips/Guards)

These are devices to clasp, clamp or hold something tightly or securely together.

A dress clip could be purely decorative or used to hold a collar in place or for a neck closure. In the 1930's, dress clips worn singly or in pairs, were favored as decorative pieces of jewelry. Most were of pot metals, studded with colored paste stones or rhinestones. These were set into varied patterns influenced by the Deco and Moderne movements. Dress clips were made in hundreds of shapes and sizes. All had clips rather than the sharp dual-pronged device of the Fur Clip or the jagged-toothed "crocodile" type opening of the Sweater Clip/Guard.

Fur Clips were most ornate and had a spring-loaded device with sharp dual-pronged pins for insertion into a thickness of fur or fabric. Both Dress and Fur clips could be worn in turbans and in fur hats.

Sweater Clips (or Sweater Guards), were two decorative and functional clips linked together by a short chain. These clips/guards could be highly decorative when worn with evening sweaters that were beaded, sequined or embroidered. The clips were clasped to an open sweater which was draped over the shoulders, thereby keeping the sweater from slipping or being lost. Clips were simple or ornate.

CLOISONNE - kloi'-zo-na (also see ENAMELLING)
A type of enamelling in which thin wire made of silver, gold, bronze or copper is gilded, then bent to form cells (*cloisons*). Each cell or *cloison* is then filled with enamel. Each color is in a separate compartment, each compartment separated by this thin wire.

COCKTAIL RING
A ring produced during the Deco epoch, which was weighty in design and material. The ring was worn at cocktail parties, dinner and after-theatre parties during the late twenties. The original dinner ring was of gold or platinum, set with magnificently cut gems. Reproductions in alloyed metals and fine foiled glass stones entered the mass production market and such rings were no longer confined to evening wear but were worn conspicuously from dawn to dusk and on into the eveing. Man-made synthetic stones, especially the "imitation diamonds", have contributed to this renewed heyday which was all the vogue in the "roarin' twenties".

COLLAR BUTTONS & STUDS
Collar buttons were made stronger and more durable than shirt studs. This is because the collar button had to fasten the collar tightly around the throat and collars of the 1925-1935 period were still being heavily starched and required a strong and durable fastening.

Parks Brothers & Rogers (Providence, RI) were makers of the "Parkroger", and advertised: "the original . . . one-piece collar button, stud and solderless cuff buttons . . . the original American Lever and Pointer collar buttons". We think of the collar button as a very simple, round shape, but it actually came in various shapes and designs. Some folded forward; some were designed with Masonic symbols and others were in a pointed shape, the point often set with a pearl or a diamond.

Collar buttons came with a long or short shank, and many of them had patented clamps to keep them from being lost or from loosening. Some of the patented clamps opened on a small spring and had meshing teeth on either side to secure the collar. It would seem that an appropriate name for this masculine device would be a "dog collar", because of its restraining "virtue". But the term "dog collar" applied only to a woman's choker piece of jewelry.

However, the collar button was not only a man's accessory but a lady's as well. Ladies' collar buttons were worn in combination sets which included the collar button, dress buttons and cuff buttons. The collar button, usually associated with men's wear, won popularity with the shirtwaist which complemented the "Gibson Girl" attire and on into those early 1925-1935 years of women's employment in banks and offices. Women had taken on the fashionable masculine accessories of collar buttons, cuff buttons and dress buttons in matching sets

made of rolled plate, gold or silver. All were engraved or highly chased with much raised edgework. A few were set with conservative, decorative, colored stones. In some instances, the matched sets included a pair of hatpins of matched design.

Dress buttons were to women what dress studs were to men. Studs were worn in front of the shirt and they were highly decorative. Shirt studs were commonly worn even into the late 1920's and early 1930's. Today, shirt studs are usually associated with the formal tuxedo or other formal attire.

COMBS
Combs did not become purely ornamental until about 1880. Before that time, they were not only decorative but functional. In the mid-twenties, the "Gibson Girl" hairdo was popular and the comb again became functional.

From 1880 to approximately 1920, the hair was arranged to present an attractive appearance from every vantage point. Therefore, there was an abundance of combs, clasps, barretts, ribbons, etc., worn at one time. No fashionable woman considered her wardrobe complete without a myriad of combs: side, pompadour, back combs and decorative ones. Combs were required for various *coiffures* such as the Greek Knot or Grecian Knot--which was a plain coil twisted or rolled low on the neck. This type of hairdo required hairpins as well as several fancy combs which were inserted for both utility and attractiveness.

Early combs were generally made of real tortoise-shell, bone, sterling, gold and ivory. After 1900, imitation materials were more popularly used, especially in America. These plastics were much less expensive to produce. However, in the late sixties, concern for endangered species such as the tortoise, elephant and tusk-bearing sea animals precluded the use of those materials in all types of adornments, including combs and jewelry. Therefore, it was not simply a matter of monetary concern, but the concern for animal species which influenced the manufacturer of modern-day combs to use the many new compositions and plastics readily available.

Back combs usually had three or more teeth and often the crest of the comb was hinged for easy insertion and more comfortable wearing. Fancy combs were set with brilliants, Bohemian garnets and other ornamental gemstones. Imitation tortoise-shell and ivory combs came under many trademarks such as: NuHorn, Tuf-E-Nuf and Stag, the latter manufactured by Noyes Comb Co., Binghamton, New York. Imitation tortoise-shell combs were manufactured by Schrader & Ehlers, (New York), makers of the "Olive Dore Combs". Early producers of the real tortoise-shell combs were Sadler Bros., So. Attleboro, MA, and the Wagner Comb Co., of New York. However, most of the more artful combs were imported from Europe.

As with most fashions, the vogue for changing hair-styles dictated the return of decorative hair articles, including some combs flashing with rhinestones or dripping with ribbons and silk flowers. Others have plastic geegaws attached to accent specific types of hair arrangements. Since the latter half of the twentieth century and especially with the production of stage and television spectaculars, hairdressers have utilized combs to stylize tresses in upswept, curly or lank updo, poodle cut, pony tail and all the dozens of other transformations of "hair raising" excitement a *coiffeur* could conjure.

CONCEITS
A term used to represent curiously contrived and fanciful jewelry, a jeweler's artifice or jeweled accessories which are quaint, artificial or have an affected conception that flatters one's vanity. To be "plumed with conceit" signifies an awareness or an eccentricity of dress.

The *Delineator* (March 1900) reported a "new high fashion" at the beginning of the century, stating that "dainty neck conceits" were becoming an important item in women's wardrobes. ". . . there is no bit of finery so truly feminine," the article stated, "or possessing so many charming possibilities as the tie or collar of ribbon, velvet, chiffon or lace . . ." Each of these "neck conceits" was fastened with an unusual and attractive brooch, which is as stylish today as at the beginning of this century.

Another neck conceit was the close-fitting "stock", a wide velvet ribbon folded around a stiffened foundation. Fastened on the side of the velvet ribbon was a jeweled ornament. The actual fastening of the ribbon was to the back, but the jewel pinned at the front gave the impression that the jewel was the clasp. This "stock" is now referred to as a "choker" or "dog collar".

The neckware of the turn of the century could change a blouse or shirtwaist into varied costumes to be worn with the close-fitting skirts of the period. The waistline of the skirt was accentuated with a small jeweled clasp that often matched the brooch worn at the neck or at the shoulder. In the 1950-1960 period, these small "conceits" were called "scatter" pins.

Millinery for all seasons was given brilliancy by some of the more elaborate creations and conceits of jewels such as dull gold enamelling in colored alloys, crystal carbochons, wide buckles of gold, cut steel and rhinestones. Added to all this were the popular hat ornaments and small and oftentimes garish-looking beaded or plastic hatpins. *Cloche* hats and turbans were made vogue-ish by the addition of a brilliant ornament or clip.

CORAL (genuine)

Skeleton of the coral polyp which was highly popular in fashionable English Victorian circles. Most coral used in Victorian jewelry came from the Mediterranean.

CRYSTAL

A colorless quartz most often implemented in cut and faceted beads, pendants and rings. Crystal, in its natural form, is not to be confused with man-made glass, although the term is used interchangeably to refer to the Austrian and Bohemian rhinestones, foiled and unfoiled faceted glass imitation gemstones. Much of the finest Austrian rhinestones contained such large quantities of lead that the stones required no foiling whatsoever to reflect a dazzling brilliance.

Czechoslovakian "sunray" crystals, made of glass, were set into silver or gold filigree manufactured as pendants, bracelets, rings and earrings. In the center of the "sun", was a small set consisting of a half-pearl or tiny diamond outlined by a tiny filigree frame. Frosted rock crystal was utilized in much Deco jewelry, combined with 20th century metals such as chrome and rhodium.

CUT STEEL (also see MARCASITE)

A metal often mistaken for marcasite. Cut steel was faceted and hand-riveted to a buckle or brooch frame. Cut and faceted steel beads were often used as spacers or decorative accents on cloth. Some cut steel was machine-made and appeared as strips or casements rather than individual sets.

DAMASCENE - dăm'-à-sèn

To inlay gold or silver into iron or steel in a decorative pattern. Characteristic of ornaments from Damascus. More recently, damascene is exported from Toledo, Spain, where the art-form seems to have reached its zenith.

DIAMONDS (also see CARAT)

A valuable gem of extreme hardness consisting of pure carbon. Usually clear and colorless, diamonds are sometimes yellow, blue, green or black.

From 1850-1900, the old mine-cut diamonds were in vogue. The "brilliant-cut" diamond has 56 or more facets and relates to more modern faceting practices which became popular after 1918. A "brilliant" cut has 88 or more facets.

In 1922, the *baguette*, (or emerald-cut) for diamonds was introduced. *Pave'*-set is probably the oldest form of setting for this gem, and was much in favor during the Art Deco period.

It is used consistently in the setting of imitation diamonds, rhinestones and brilliants in high fashion costume jewelry -- especially in the 1940's-1960's (see *Pave'*). 1940 saw square and rectangular cuts; 1950, the *marquise*.

The emphasis on creative gem-cutting was evident during the exhibit held in 1946 at the New York *Museum of Modern Art*. Further interest was heightened by the premier of "Diamond U.S.A. Awards" (1954) sponsored by DeBeers Consolidated Mines, Ltd. During the 1950's, the *marquise* and pear cuts dominated the field and these cuts, accentuated by many facets, were imitated in crystal and rhinestone fashionable costume jewelry.

DIE STAMPING

To cut a design into metal for mass production and reproduction. This superseded handwrought and custom-made molds and handmade jewelry. Today, prohibitive labor costs of mold-making and casting have caused this process to become a lost art in mass-produced jewelry in the competitive market. Almost all costume jewelry is now die-stamped.

DEPOSE - dė-pōz'

A French word similar to U.S. "copyright" or "patent". The word is sometimes stamped on an article implying the article is meant for export or is imported.

DRAGON'S BREATH

Simulated Mexican fire opals, made of glass, popular from 1910 through the 1930's.

DRESS CLIP (see CLIPS)

EARRINGS

Earrings are rather easily dated. The earliest were lightweight, hollow-gold and were made with wire hooks which went through pierced ear lobes. Wire posts were made after 1900. From 1900-1930 came screw-backs and after 1930, the ear clip was introduced. Fancy "pierceless" eardrops gained popularity after 1930. Prior to 1930, most women wore pierced earrings, primarily studs and/or short drops. However, during the Art Deco period, the more daring wore elongated designs simply dripping with marcasites and imitation stones. In the 1970's, ear-piercing became the rage, resulting in a renewed interest in dangling, opulent, fashionable earrings.

EBONY

The word in Hebrew, (*eben*), signifies a **stone**, because ebony wood is hard and heavy. Ebony is a black colored wood of great hardness, heavier than water and capable of taking on a fine polish. It is found primarily in Ceylon and is used in making beads and in combination with other materials such as silver and gemstones combined in Deco jewelry artifacts.

ELECTROPLATING (or Electro-Plating)

This plating is achieved by immersing jewelry into an electro-magnetic acid bath which deposits a thin layer of gold, silver or other metal on to a lesser metal, such as nickle or pewter. The lesser metals used by jewelers are referred to as "pot metal", "base metal", "white metal" or "jeweler's metal".

EMERALD

Commonly dark green, it is also found in varied shades of green. An "emerald-cut" stone is oblong or square-cut, and is the usual cutting for a genuine emerald. Emerald-cut was introduced in the 1920's, with the vital interest in Cubism.

ENAMEL (also see *BASSE-TAILLE, CHAMPLEVE, CLOISONNE, LIMOGES, NIELLO, PILIQUE-A-JOUR* and *GUILLOCHE*)

Enamelling is a firing of melted glass. The powdered glass

mixture is composed of feldspar, quartz, soda, borax, calcium phosphates and kaolin. Metallic oxides produce the various desired colors. There is little **transparent**, see-through, colorless enamelling; rather a better and more definitive term is "translucent". However, the word "transparent" has been an accepted term for *plique-a-jour* enamelling which permits light to pass through as in stained glass.

There are several important types of enamelling:

Basse-Taille - Metal plate cut to various depths into which translucent enamel is poured, thus achieving a 3-dimensional effect. The depth of relief produces shadings from light to dark. The deeper the metal is cut, the darker the color; where shallow routing occurs, the shading is almost transparent. This routing is worked *intaglio*, the opposite of *repousse*.

Champleve - An enamelling technique in which areas of metal are hand cut, etched or routed and filled with enamel. Unlike *cloisonne*, the cells are cut rather than formed by wires. *Champleve* is most commonly applied to copper or bronze. The metals are gilded on exposed and visible surfaces.

Guilloche technique differs in that the designs are machine-turned and etched, and then enameled. This is a much faster process and many boxed sets of hatpins, matching stud buttons, buckles, brooches and medallions are representative of this technique. *Guilloche* pattern consists of interlacing curved lines.

Cloisonne - Enamelling in which thin wire of silver, gold, bronze or copper is bent to form cells, (*cloisons*), and then filled with enamel. Each color is in a separate compartment, each compartment separated by thin wire that has often been gilded.

Limoges enamel - A colorful application of enamel which depicts a portrait or scene similar to that rendered on canvas.

Niello enamelling - The lines or incisions of a design are contrasted with the color of the metal, i.e., gold, silver, etc., by applying in several layers a mixture of sulphur, lead, silver and copper. This addition appears black when filled into the engraved metallic work. *Niello* is a blackish enamelling process, providing contrasts in highlights and darkness of the design.

Plique-a-Jour - A translucent *cloisonne* in which there is no metal backing for the enamel work. During firing, a metal supportive base is used until firing ceases. Then, when the piece has cooled and the enamel has hardened, the finished product no longer requires the base, so this support is removed. It is a most cautious procedure, requiring highly skilled craftsmanship and technique.

ENGRAVING

Cutting lines into metal which are either decorative or symbolic. Method used in monogramming a crest, *cartouche*, or escutcheon.

ESCUTCHEON - ĕs-kŭch'-ŭn

Small metal plate used atop an ornament or ring, for monogram or signet.

FACET

Small flat surface cut into gemstone, glass or shell. Its purpose is to refract light or enhance the design.

FAUX - fō

Literally, the word means "false light". Used in the context of jewelry, it specifically means that the gems or gemstones reflect a "false light", in that the brilliance is achieved by highly faceted glass and foiled backing. Fashion jewelry of the finest quality can be described as being set with *faux* turquoise, rubies, emeralds or sapphires. Usually the glass stones are of the finest quality and could "pass" for the genuine article.

FESTOON

A garland of chain or chains decorated with ornamental drops or pendants which lay on a curve against a woman's up-

per bosom or draped across a man's chest. A *chatelaine* chain could well be worn in festoon fashion, meaning it would be draped from shoulder to shoulder, forming a curve at the center fall.

FILIGREE

To apply thread-like wire and decorate into a lace, lattice or cobweb work.

FIN de SIECLE - fin' dĕ sēal - (French, meaning "end-of-the-century")

This is a popular expression in art, fashion, society and in describing high fashion jewelry, denoting "decadence" or restlessness. It can also mean daring or *avant garde* -- providing a more flattering definition: "ahead of its time".

FINDINGS

Metal parts used by jewelers for finishing an ornament or attaching an ornament to a pin or link.

FLEUR-de-LIS - flûr'-dĕ-lĕ

This is the jeweler's mark for the city of Verdun, France. The term means "Flower of light". The *fleur-de-lis* is the French symbol of life and power and is designed from nature's Iris. This symbol is found on many Victorian, Edwardian and *Art Nouveau* pieces of jewelry and has been carried out in modern jewelry designs as well.

FOBS

The terms "fobs" and "charms" were interchangeable from mid-1850 through the 1930's. Watch fobs or watch charms were in vogue in the 1890's through the turn of the century and certainly on into the 1930's when the pocket watch became more popular than ever. The fobs were very desirable in agate, hematite, tiger eye, lava stone, convex crystal, goldstone, inlaid onyx and assorted onyx.

FOIL

Silver, gold or other color thin leaf of metal used to back imitation gemstones or faceted glass to improve their color and provide greater brilliance.

FRAME (see MOUNTINGS)

"FRENCH IVORY" (also see CELLULOID, BAKELITE and PLASTIC)

An imitation of ivory tusk in grained Celluloid or plastic. "French Ivory" is a registered trademark. Other ivory imitations, not quite as good, were **Ivorette, Ivorine, Ivory Pyralin,** and **DuBarry Pyralin.** In the 1870's, there was a shortage of ivory for billiard balls and a $10,000 prize was offered to anyone who could produce a substitute. John Wesley Hyatt mixed nitric acid and cellulose (guncotton), to make Celluloid. It was the first plastic to look like ivory. "French Ivory" products were produced by J.B. Ash Co. (Rockford, Illinois). Since Celluloid was highly flammable, it was eventually replaced with Bakelite and other fire-retardent plastics.

"FRENCH JET"

This is a black glass meant to imitate the natural element --JET. The name "French Jet", is a misnomer, for it is actually glass mainly from Bohemia (Czech.). It is a term which takes in almost all black sets, other than genuine jet and onyx.

FUR CLIP (see CLIPS)

GEMS and GEMSTONES

Genuine gems and gemstones are created by natural mysterious forces.

Traditionally, the gems designated as "precious" are: diamond, ruby, sapphire and emerald. All other stones are considered gemstones or ornamental gems. The term "semi-precious" is considered obsolete. The modern view is that all gems are "precious" according to individual taste or preference. However, the **value** of the traditionally classified precious gems are usually far greater than the other natural stones. Therefore, "gemstones" is the word used when referring to gems other than the diamond, the ruby, the sapphire and the emerald.

The faceted portion of a gem or gemstone -- the top of the stone -- is called the "table". The bottom of the stone is called the "pavillion". The point or the center is known as the "culet".

For many centuries past, jewels were considered medicinal. It was believed that some stones possessed unquestioned healing power. Hebrew tradition states that the Tablets of Moses were of sapphire, and the Hebrew word "sappir" means "the most beautiful". It also symbolizes loyalty, justice, beauty and nobility. Hence the "royal blue" or "purple of nobility".

Emeralds from India, Persia and Columbia (South America) are most valuable. Emeralds are shown as the emblem of charity, hope, joy and abundance. It also has the reputation of curing epilepsy and being an all-around pain killer. St. John writes of the emerald in his Apocalypse.

The diamond has always been regarded as the most precious stone. It was believed that if a guilty person wore a diamond, it turned red; but in the presence of innocence it would retain its original purity and brilliance. The diamond was reputed to be a preserver against epidemics and poisons, that it calmed anger and formented conjugal love. The ancients called it "the stone of reconciliation". It symbolizes constancy, strength and innocence.

In ancient times, the opal was considered a splendid stone, but due to the belief that it attracted misfortune, it had the effect of lowering the desirability of the stone except by those who were born in October. This, of course, was a mere superstition seemingly founded on a Russian legend that had come into France. It was reported that the Empress Eugenie had a horror of the opal and at the sight of one in the *Tuillaries*, she was actually terrorized.

The language of gems, their signficance and the superstitions connected with gems and gemstones have been documented in great depth in many books on stones and lapidary work. In fact, whole volumes have been written about the curiosity of gems, gems as talismans, the lore of gems and so forth. It is another fascinating aspect of jewelry which deserves avid pursuit.

It is always fashionable among lovers and friends to note the significance attached to various gems and gemstones, and to give these as birthday, engagement and wedding remembrances.

Birthstones and Their Significance

Month	Stone (Modern v. Ancient)	Significance
January	Garnet (unchanged)	Insures constancy, true friendship, fidelity.
February	Amethyst (formerly included Pearl)	Freedom from passion and from care.
March	Aquamarine (formerly Bloodstone)	Courage, wisdom, firmness in affection.
April	Diamond (unchanged)	Emblem of innocence and purity.
May	Emerald (unchanged)	Discovers false friends and insures true love.
June	Pearl (formerly Agate or Cat's Eye)	Insures long life, health and prosperity.
July	Ruby (formerly included Coral)	Discovers poison, corrects evils resulting from mistaken friendship.
August	Peridot (formerly Sardonyx or Moonstone)	Without it, no conjugal felicity, so must live unloved and alone.
September	Sapphire (formerly included Chrysolite)	Frees from evil passions and sadness of the mind.
October	Opal (unchanged)	Denotes hope and sharpens the sight and faith of the possessor.
November	Topaz (unchanged)	Fidelity and friendship. Prevent bad dreams.
December	Turquoise (unchanged, but additions of Lapis Lazuli and/or Blue Zircon)	Success and prosperity in love.

The language of gems and gemstones has changed in modern times. From the earliest of times, jewelry was worn primarily by men, and the gems and gemstones formerly related to birth-month were more popular with them than with women who began to wear "jewelry for the masses" after the turn of the century.

Jewels and Anniversaries

Twelfth anniversary	Agate
Thirteenth anniversary	Moonstone
Seventeenth anniversary	Amethyst
Eighteenth anniversary	Garnet
Thirtieth anniversary	Pearl
Thirty-fifth anniversary	Coral
Fortieth anniversary	Ruby
Forty-fifth anniversary	Sapphire
Fifty-fifth anniversary	Emerald
Sixtieth anniversary	Diamond

GERMAN SILVER

Metal which has no actual silver content but is an alloy of copper, zinc and nickel with the highest content being nickel which gives it a silvery-white color. It is a common base for plating. Also called "nickle silver", "french grey" or "gun metal".

GILT (or Gilded)

A method used after the invention of electro-gilding. Gilding (gilt) is a process of plating a die-stamped piece of base metal to give it a real or psuedo gold or silver color. Most often, and more abundant, are gold color ornaments which have been gilded, rather than **silver-color** gilt. Most fashion or costume jewelry is rhodium plated, rather than silver gilt. Gilding is considered inferior to rolled plate or electroplating.

GOLD (also see CARAT/KARAT)

Precious metal ore containing alloys which vary depending on desired color and hardness.

Gold colors range from green to dull yellow, to bright pink and even red. White color (the color of platinum or silver) is achieved by alloying nickel and a small percentage of platinum to gold. Thus, **white gold** is an alloy of gold with silver, palladium, platinum or nickle.

Platinum is more a 20th Century metal and is represented in jewelry after the turn of the century, particularly used during the Art Deco period.

Gold is twice as heavy as silver, which is perhaps the reason why a more **solid** silver was used while gold was plated, filled or rolled with inferior alloys. Platinum is even heavier than gold, which explains why it was not used for early baroque pieces.

The term **carat** or **karat** is for the fineness of gold. Example: 18K or 750=18/24 or 750/1000th, representing 75% pure gold content.

GOLD ELECTROPLATE (see ELECTROPLATING)

GOLD-FILLED

Joining a layer or layers of gold alloy to a base metal alloy, then rolling or drawing out as required for thickness or thin sheeting of material.

GOLDSTONE

Man-made brown glass with specs of copper infused within, made as an imitation of Adventurine gemstone which contains particles of gold-colored minerals.

GRANULAR WORK

Gold or silver metal applied in decorative designs which resemble tiny grains or pin-heads, roundly shaped.

"GLASGOW FOUR"

Consisted of C.R. Mackintosh, Herbert McNair and the sisters Margaret and Frances MacDonald, to whom they were wed. Although Mackintosh and McNair worked in the Celtic style, rather than in the "high" *Art Nouveau* of the French, their designs greatly influenced the modern movement in Austria, Belgium and Germany. However, when it came to jewelry, it was their wives who were most productive and influential to both their husbands' work and the art of "modern" jewelry. Their work was vital right through the Art Deco and Art Moderne periods.

GYPSY SETTING (also known as Bezel)

A type of setting where the top of the stone is exposed just above the metal casing.

GUILLOCHE' - gĭ-losh' (see ENAMEL)

HAIR ORNAMENTS (also see COMBS and BARRETT)

Hair ornaments have existed even in early tribal cultures. Early hair ornaments were functional as well as decorative, providing a pick used for cleaning and separating tangles in the hair. Hair ornaments preceded the invention of primitive combs. Once combs came into being, hair ornamentation became symbolic and ornamental.

From 1850 through the 1925 era, hair ornaments were made in high *baroque* style in both gold and sterling silver. Most of the metal was cut, pierced or engraved with some fine *repousse* work. The entire ornament, including the teeth, were of inlaid ivory, bone and tortoise. From 1910-1930, hair ornaments were made of either Celluloid or plastics embedded with brilliants.

Ordinarily, hair ornaments have simply a stem or pair of teeth, whereas combs have as many as four to nine teeth, depending on the size and style of the comb. Atop the stem or pair of teeth, is the ornamental decoration used to enhance the hairstyle and fashionable dress. Although delegated to the attic after the 1950's, hair ornaments are once more in style, lending a touch of glamour and femininity to the wardrobe.

HAIR PINS

The **Tortoise Brand** trademark was that of Rice & Hochster Makers (New York), a firm manufacturing three shapes of hair pins: straight, loop and crimped. They sold for $.25 per dozen boxes in the 1920's-1930's and were available in three colors: shell, amber and black. Hair pins come in various lengths from 1″-3″, and in several gauges of wire.

Hair pins were made of rolled gold decorated with birds, butterflies and stars and these were worn in great profusion throughout the headdress. In 1921, Swartchild & Co. (Chicago) advertised in their catalogue "The Neverslip Hairpin" for holding an eyeglass-chain securely to the hair. The chain extended from the curve of the hair pin to the small loop at the side of the spectacles or eye glasses.

HALLMARK

An official mark first adopted in England. The mark is incised, punched or stamped on gold or silver to show quality and to signify purity of metal according to "sterling" or "carat" standard. Other countries' hallmarks indicate origin, patent, manufacture, etc. Most of the countries in Europe stamped their gold and silver wares with "hallmarks". As early as 1363, England had already passed laws stating that every master goldsmith shall have a "quote by himself", and the same mark "shall be known by them which shall be assigned by the King to survey their work allay". That meant all goldsmiths' work had to be assayed before they could be marked by the king's authority. Such individual marks would certify the ore content of both gold and silver.

By 1857, the word "Sterling" became universally used except in the United States. Until 1894, no State protection was given in the United States to purchases of either gold or silver, and the buyer could only trust the reputation of the maker and dealer.

State laws regulating the stamping of the words "Sterling", "Sterling Silver", "Coin", or "Coin Silver" on wares of silver or metals purporting to be silver, were first passed in 1894. Massachusetts was the leader in this regard, but many other states followed suit within the next decade. These laws were similar within each state and they specified that any wares which were marked "Sterling" or "Sterling Silver", must contain 925 parts of the fine silver in every 1,000 parts. "Coin" or "Coin Silver", were to contain 900 parts of fine silver in every 1,000. Persons were subject to misdemeanor charges if they attempted to sell merchandise marked "Sterling" or "Coin Silver" that did not contain the lawful quantities of pure silver.

Regarding the hallmarking of gold: it had become law that no article was to be offered for sale that did not plainly stamp the exact number of twenty-fourth parts of pure gold or portion of gold the article actually contained. Any person found guilty of violation of the provisions of this act could be fined up to $1,000, or imprisoned in a "common jail" (not to exceed one year or both), "at the discretion of the court".

Hallmarking became so strict that even portions of a particular piece of jewelry had to be marked. For instance, the front of a pin could be marked "Sterling"; but if only the **front** was sterling, the back would be stamped thus: "**Sterling front**".

Trademarks should not be confused with **hallmarks**. A trademark is the name of a manufacturing company or of the artisan. A hallmark is a guarantee of the quality of the ore contained in the merchandise.

Mass production brought new codes, and many European countries then allowed their **retailers** of jewelry to have their own mark. Therefore, many manufacturers, craftsmen, designers and/or artists, remain unknown. Retailers oftentimes left the jewelry unmarked, except for hallmarking and placed their own identity (name of retail outlet or advertising slogan) on fancy jewel boxes made especially for the trade. Liberty & Co. (England) is a prime example. Their artists and jewelers were compelled to remain anonymous, and all the "modern works" and "Orientalia" were marked or labeled with the Liberty & Co. trademark. Tiffany & Co. (New York) is another example where fine jewelers remained anonymous, except for a few proteges who developed a following of their own and built on their own reputation. In many instances, jewelers who designed and manufactured mass produced jewelry for department store trade became actual "jobbers" and the backbone of a multi-million dollar industry.

In a 1980 survey taken from the ''Yellow Pages'' nation-wide, there were no less than 5,000 jewelry wholesalers, and more than 36,000 jewelry retailers. Yet in the high fashion jewelry manufacturer/designer category, there are fewer than 100 recognized names in the entire industry. This book is one small step toward recognizing a fruitful industry and providing some archival record of the achievements and accomplishments. The pictorial record herein serves as a chronical for historical reference or jewelry journal reporting about a fifty year period when advanced technology and high costs of labor were no stumbling blocks to fine cast molds, hand tooling and hand setting, the true hallmark of 1925-1975 fashion jewelry.

Marks Mistaken For Name of Manufacturer/Designer/Jeweler

R.P. = rolled gold or silver plate
E.P. = gold or silver electroplate
G.F. = gold filled (usually preceded by numeral, i.e. 14K G.F. or 10K G.F.)
N.S. = nickle silver
G.S. = German silver
B.M. = Britannia metal
W.M. = White metal
G.E.P. = Gold electro-plate

HAT PIN (also see HATPIN)

A man's decorative pin worn on a hat, cap and particulary in recent times as an insignia on hats worn by both men and women in the armed forces. Hat pins have also become collector's items, especially those of political campaigns or Olympic commemoratives. The hat pin is unlike a woman's **hatpin** (one word), a pinning device absolutely necessary to securely pin ones hat to the hair and head. A hat pin has been worn in men's hats from the earliest of times to designate his so-called ''station in life'', his religious order, his peerage, family crest and so forth. HATS and HAT PINS are given much archival information in the titles mentioned under HATPIN (below).

HATPIN

The author has written the first world-wide definitive work on the subject of hatpins, titled: *The Collector's Encyclopedia of Hatpins and Hatpin Holders*, published by Collector Books (1976). Now out-of-print and being revised, a supplemental work was published by Collector Books (1983), titled: *Hatpins and Hatpin Holders: An Illustrated Value Guide.* This latter book is available to readers seeking a fascinating story about this functional, decorative, historical and political piece of jewelry--the hatpin. The woman's device is spelled as HATPIN (one word), so as to differentiate from a man's hat pin, which was worn for decorative purposes and as a means of identity. *The Encyclopedia Brittanica* has recently accepted this definition.

HEMATITE - hĕm´-à-tīt

A blood-like red iron ore, in the form of crystals, used primarily as settings for men's jewelry. Brown hematite, called limonite in modern-day usage, refers to either the reddish-brown or the brown color.

ILLUSION SETTING

A setting in which the stone is made to appear larger by cutting metal in shape of the gem-table, thus giving the stone the illusion of being a heavier carat.

IMITATION (also see SYNTHETICS)

To make out of other materials a substance resembling the natural elements, i.e., paste or rhinestones for gems; hard rubber, dyed and then molded into coral-color flowers; plastic tortoise shell; ''French Ivory'', an imitation of ivory, bone, etc. **Imitation is not** the same as **synthetic.**

INTAGLIO - ĭn-tăl´-yō

To cut a design deeply on the obverse or front side of a gem or other type material. *Intaglio* is the opposite of *repousse* work done in metals.

IRIDESCENT

To give a high luster to glass or other man-made materials. Some gems and gemstones have a natural iridescent quality peculiar to some stones. However, relating to natural gems and gemstones, such refraction is usually referred to as ''brilliance'' or ''luster'', rather than iridescent. This is particularly true of pearls.

JADE

A hard stone with a resinous or oily aspect when polished. Jade is not actually carved but is cut or chipped, chiseled, or ground into the desired size and shape, then polished. Jade is found in many shades and the presence of quantities of iron determine the color. The colors vary: mutton fat (sometimes streaked with gray or brown tones); green (spinach or moss colors); celadon (off-white color); tangerine; pink; lavender; and the most desirable color, luminous apple-green called Imperial Jade.

Jade is formed into amulets, hair ornaments, rings, bracelets, beads, necklaces, pendants, and Chinese burial pieces called ''weights'' for the tongue and eyes of the deceased.

Because jade is a tough, hard, resilient stone, it cannot be easily scratched, whereas imitation jade (called by many new names), **can** be scratched. One of the most common imitations of jade is dyed calcite, which is nothing more than ordinary marble, chalk or limestone.

Although jade occurs in Asia, America and other countries, the Oriental jade is most desirable -- and plentiful in its more common varieties.

Nephrite jade (white to dark green) is found on mainland China. Jadeite (emerald to pale green, white, red-brown, yellow-brown, violet & pink) is from Burma.

JAPANNED

Japanning is a process of darkening iron wire by immersing the wire into black japan, a by-product of coal. Japanned metals were introduced particularly for mourning jewelry mountings, including the pinning devices.

JAPONISM - jăp´ ō-nĭz´-m

Japanese influence in the art of *cloisonne* enamelling, lacquer work and other Oriental wares, using plant motifs and curving lines which highly influenced the European *Art Nouveau* artisans. Characteristic of Japonism is two-dimensional graphics, quality of art, structure and expression in simplest of context. This influence prevailed on into the Deco and Moderne periods, too.

''JARGOW-NIB''

A nickname used in 1913 for point protectors. Named for Berlin's police-president, von Jargold, who sought to enforce the wearing of hatpin ''safeties'' by law. The first report of the ''Jargow-nib'' was in the **New York Times**, April 19, 1913. ''Nibs'' were included in the sale of hatpins and hat ornaments and woman's scarf pins, and in many States the laws prohibiting the length of hatpins and the use of ''safety-nibs'' are still on the books. Even to this day, women's scarf pins and hat ornaments come equipped with a safety ''nib'' -- safe keeping, and to keep from being stuck by the pinpoint. Details about the legal ramifications are in Baker's encyclopedic work and supplemental work on hatpins. (see **HATPINS**).

JET (Genuine and Imitation)

Jet is the name given most black jewelry whether it be genuine or glass. **Genuine jet will retain its sparkling polish for** many years. "Black glass" (also known as "French Jet", even though most black glass came from Bohemia), will crack, scratch and become dull.

Genuine jet is a brown-black lignite in which the texture or grain of the original fossilized wood comprised of coal, can still be seen. The finest genuine jet comes from Whitby, England, where over 200 workshops produced Victorian Era jewelry. Jet was, at that time, associated strictly with mourning, although it had been worn in earlier times as decorative jewelry. Jet jewelry was considered proper wear during the first year of mourning, then diamonds or pearls were allowable during the second period of mourning. During those first two years, a widow was expected to wear "widow's weeds" and at that time, no earrings were worn in the street. This was the etiquette, c. 1850-1900. In some religious households, the wearing of mourning-black clothing was strictly adhered to. Because a period of mourning was imposed even at the death of a distant relative, no less a husband, parent or child, some women spent their entire adult lives dressed in either black, grey or deep purple.

The Art Deco period featured black and white geometric patterns, making black glass popular again for joyful renditions of Art Deco and Moderne jewelry.

American Indians of the Southwest used genuine American jet in jewelry, which they call "Apache tears". Beads called "black amber" are usually black glass beads.

JEWELERS (1925-1935)

For biographical information about some of the noteworthy Art Deco and Art Moderne jewelers, artisans, designers, manufacturers and retailers of this genre of jewelry, refer to the author's book, *Art Nouveau and Art Deco Jewelry*. Published by Collector Books (1981).

KARAT (see CARAT)

LAPIS LAZULI - lăp'-is lăz'-ŭ-li

Deep blue gemstone, sometimes containing gold-colored specks of iron pyrites. Horn, stone or jasper are all sometimes artificially colored to look like genuine Lapis.

LAVALIERE - lăv'-à-lēr'

Named for the Duchess de La Valliere, mistress of Louis XIV. This type of jewelry is an ornament hanging from a chain worn around the neck. The terms *"lavaliere"* and "pendant" could be used interchangeably. However, *"lavaliere"* does not appear in jewelers' catalogues until after 1900. Pendants and *lavalieres* have small jump rings or fancy type loops through which a chain is threaded.

LIMOGES - lĕ-mōzh' (enamel)

A colorful application of enamel depicting a portrait or scene similar to those rendered on canvas.

LOCKETS

These ornaments hung from neck chains and bracelets and were also worn as charms or fobs. They were designed in ovals, rounds, hearts and other varied shapes. Lockets opened to hold one, two and often three or more pictures, as well as mementoes such as pressed flowers or a lock of hair. They were embossed, chased, engraved, enamelled or die-stamped for mass production. Many were set with gems and gemstones or had pictorial, floral or other motifs wrought in *repousse* work.

Lockets were made of gold, silver, rolled gold and plate. The gold-front lockets for gentlemen, worn with their waist or vest chains, were larger and much more intricately worked and designed than those made for women. The solid gold front of the locket accepted high relief and design work and were usually accented with a gem or two. Rubies, pearls and sapphires were highly favored. These were accentuated by a scenic engraving or portrait. The chased frames and edges of the lockets were finished with lovely chasing.

Lockets from 1890 through WWII were probably the most sentimental gift for men, women and children. To this day, the locket remains a highly prized piece of heirloom jewelry.

LORGNETTE - lôr'-nyĕt'

A *lorgnette* is a pair of eye-glasses or an opera glass which is attached to a handle. A *lorgnon* is actually a single glass such as a monocle, but ordinarily speaking, *lorgnon* could be a substitute word for *lorgnette*.

Most *lorgnons* fold, and there were tiny ones especially made for *chatelaines*. Some were so small, they were called "glove lorgnons".

Frames for *lorgnettes* could be simple or ornate. Some were jewel encrusted or encased in tortoise-shell or mother-of-pearl. Some had crests engraved in solid gold. Shell and horn, however, were the best sellers and were made by European craftsmen.

There were wrist chains used especially for the glove *lorgnon*. Chains and *lorgnons* frequently go together and the same decorative treatment was usually applied to both. In 1880, *lorgnettes* made of zylonite (plastic) were offered for sale.

The *Art Nouveau* period produced exquisite *lorgnettes* which folded in half on a small hinge and could slide into the handle. The demise of the *lorgnette* came with the Great Depression of the 1930's, when theatres and other places of luxury were less frequented. The sobering event dictated a less "affected" stance by high society in face of mass poverty. The Art Deco period (1925-1930) produced an interesting display of plastic *lorgnettes*, with geometric designs studded with rhinestones and artificial glass gems. These plastic *lorgnettes* were lighter in weight than the metallic counterparts, and these were stylishly worn on silk cords.

MARCASITE

A white iron pyrite. If the ore is yellow, it takes on the appearance of "fool's gold". Cut steel jewelry and marcasites resemble one another in color and faceted treatment, but cut steel rusts easily and is not as hard nor as brilliant as natural marcasites. Most marcasite jewelry is made in France and is usually mounted in sterling silver, although marcasites were also set into tortoise shell or plastic. Individually mounted marcasites are more desirable than machine-made casements or strips for mass-produced settings.

MARQUISE CUT - mår-kēz'

Popular cut for diamonds in which the stone is brilliantly faceted. The diamond's oval shape is gradually narrowed until opposite ends are pointed.

MATRIX

An inferior or foreign substance that intrudes in or surrounds a gemstone such as Turquoise or Lapis Lazuli.

MEDALS and BADGES

Given for prizes and testimonals, they came in many shapes and designs. There are medals for rowing, tennis, baseball, gun clubs, bicycling, shooting, bowling and athletics. It is noted in various catalogues printed after 1900, that to the aforementioned awards were added: scholarship, music, good conduct, society, special prize, prize essay and art.

Most medals and badges were intricately engraved and enameled, many with escutcheons carrying the Heraldic Crest or a monogram of the donor. The recipient's name, date and the occasion were engraved on the reverse side of the medals and badges.

Medals could be worn from a chain, whereas badges were more often associated with the type pinned to a lapel, shirtwaist or uniform. Badges were often sewn on various color ribbons, measuring from ½" to 3" in length. Fastening pins with clasps were then inserted at one end of the ribbon, and the badge hung from there.

Hat badges, or hat pins, are worn by men. Hatpins are worn by women. (See HATPINS).

MEDALLIONS (see CHARMS or FOBS)

Shaped like a medal, from which it derives its name. In treatment, it is more likely to be more highly engraved and larger in size than either a medal, charm or fob.

MEMORIAL JEWELRY (see MOURNING JEWELRY)

MEN'S JEWELRY (see CHAINS, COLLAR BUTTONS and STICKPINS)

Jeweled and metallic adornments for men originated in ancient times. As in nature, it was the male who decorated his body with attractive shells, wooden beads, bronze and gold. The earliest jewelry was worn by men, not women. Even as late as the 19th Century, buttons, brooches, hat pins, stickpins, watch fobs, knives, snuff box pendants and many other silver and gold implements were the conceits of men. Watch chains were especially prized until World War I, when the wrist watch was first introduced.

After World War I, the fancy cravat was replaced by a tie, fastened with a tight knot and held in place by a tie clip. Many of these were ornately engraved and accented with jewels. Conservative cuff links and shirt studs were fashionable until after World War II, when a rash of new designer shirts with large French cuffs appeared in vogue. These were enhanced with no-holds-barred cuff links ranging from ultra-simplicity to ultra-simpleton designs.

During World War II, Billikens carved by Eskimos in walrus ivory, were purchased by the military stationed at Marks Field (near Nome, Alaska), and carried as good luck charms or worn as tie-tacs under a uniform collar.

The height of popularity for opulent tie bars and cuff links occurred during the 1960s-1970s, with companies such as Avon, Emmons, Sarah Coventry, Beaucraft, Anson, Hickok (makers of designer belt buckles), Taunton (makers of "Clipper" men's jewelry) and Speidel producing a huge assortment of men's jewelry accessories.

The late 1970's and early 1980's re-introduced the centuries-old fashion of men wearing neck-chains, bracelets, pinning devices and several rings worn on both hands. Today, even men who consider themselves "conservative" have thrown open the shirt-collar to display one or more neck-chains, with or without pendants. Whereas early noblemen carried "purses", modern men carry leather "pouches".

Men's jewelry, from ancient to modern times, is a subject diversified enough to fill an encyclopedic work of its own. It is a genre of jewelry which is not only decorative but has historical significance beginning with the Bible, on to "crown jewels", and modern investments in gold and diamonds.

For additional photographs and information about **Men's Jewelry**, read Baker's book *One Hundred Years of Collectible Jewelry: 1850-1950* (Collector Books).

MILLEFIORI - mĭl′ ė-fi̇-ŏ-rė

Multi-colored mosaic beads requiring great skill of the glassblower to create florals, animals and intricate designs. **Millefiori** is most familiar in paperweights. Glass beads were manufactured in Italy, primarily in Murano, which produced highly prized Venetian glass beads.

MINE CUT (or Old Mine Cut)

Gems from South America, mostly Brazil, before diamond mines were discovered in Africa. The cut differs from "European cut" in that it is thicker from the table to the culet (the bottom facet) and the point (or culet) is cut off flat. Mine cut diamonds are *passe'*, and the brilliant cut with 58 or more facets remains the better accepted and appreciated cut for diamonds and other gems.

MOONSTONE

A translucent gemstone with a pearly or opaline luster.

MOSAIC

Creating a motif or design parquetry with minute pieces of colored glass or stone which have been set into plaster. Individual portions of the design are sectioned by metal, similar to the form used in *cloisonne* enamelling. This type of Venetian jewelry work is also called *pietra dura*, and was utilized for such designs as foliage, leaves, flowers, pebbles, etc. In *pietra dura*, the mosaic design is usually set in dull jet or black marble. Complete mosaics are mounted in gilded brass frames, some with fancy edgework.

MOTHER-OF-PEARL

Differs from abalone in color in that Mother-of-Pearl is the iridescent inner-shell layer of a pearly oyster.

MOUNTING

A specific adaptation of a stone or artifact within a cage, frame, or setting comprised of various metals, wood or plastic.

MOURNING JEWELRY

Black jewelry, either real or imitation jet, black onyx, ebony or bog oak. It was popularized during Queen Victoria's long period of mourning (1861-1901), upon the death of her Prince Consort, Albert.

Onyx and jet were the stones most widely worn for mourning jewelry even through the 1930's.

A fine source book for Victorian symbolism, the language of lovers, mourning jewelry and love brooches, is *Victorian Sentimental Jewelry*, by Diana Cooper.

NECKLACES (see *LAVALIERE*, PENDANTS, CHARMS, and BEADS)

NIBS (also see JARGOW-NIBS)

Small metal sheaths into which the pointed end of a pin can be inserted, thereby affording protection against "pin pricks", and against loss.

NIELLO - ni-el′-ō (enamelling)

The lines or incisions of a design are contrasted with the color of the metal, i.e., gold, silver, etc., by applying in several layers a mixture of sulphur, lead, silver and copper, which appears black after being filled into the engraved metallic work. Quite simply, *niello* enamelling is a blackish enamel work.

NODDER (also called "Bobbler", "Springer", "Trembler" or "Tremblant")

A short spring which causes an ornamental head to bobble or bounce freely. Several short springs or wires could be utilized on a bouquet of metallic flowers set with brilliants. The ornament would sparkle as it moved and caught the light. Figural animals, birds and flowers had spring devices which would cause the head, feet or blooms to bobble in motion.

OPALESCENCE

A pearly sheen radiating from within a gem such as a moonstone. Mexican fire opals, made of foiled glass, imitated opals by seemingly giving off this radiation "from within".

OPENWORK (see PIERCEWORK)

PARURE - på-rŏŏr′

Matching jewelry containing three or more pieces such as a necklace, choker, brooch, earrings, bracelet and ring. *Demi-parure* consists of only two or three matching sets, but the modern term for matched jewelry consisting of two to three pieces is a **set**.

PASTE

A superior glass containing oxide of lead used for jewelry to imitate gems and gemstones. Joseph Strass perfected paste, although paste was used since ancient times as imitations of precious stones. Much paste is actually a composition of pounded rock crystal melted with alkaline salts and colored with metallic oxides.

Some paste stones are set with bright foil, a thin leaf of metal placed in back of a glass stone to heighten its brilliance. The finest quality paste, however, requires no foil or backing and is usually claw-set or bezel mounted as if it were the genuine article. Inferior paste may be backed with mercury or quicksilver and applied by machine rather than the more expensive handwork which requires each paste stone to be individually mounted. Commercial pastes are molded. Unless one is an expert, the superior pastes of today are sometimes difficult to distinguish between diamonds, spinels or other imitated gems.

PATE-de-VERRE - pä/tă-dè-var (Paste Glass)

Crystal and lead combined in a pulverized heavy paste compound which is then layered in a mold and kiln-fired. After cooling, the mold is broken. The result is a unique object rendered in muted hues of heavy glass.

PAVE′ SET - pă-va′

Stones placed so closely together that almost no metal shows between them. This was a favored type of setting for rhinestones c. 1950-1960.

PEACOCK EYE GLASS

A glass whose coloring resembles the "eye" of a peacock's feather.

PEARLS (also see WAX BEAD PEARL and BLISTER PEARL)

Pearls are the natural formation of a secretion called nacre. This nacre lies within an oyster and is caused by some irritating substance such as a grain of sand. When the pearls are naturally formed, they are called **Oriental** pearls. Cultured pearls are made by nature with the help of man. This man-induced process originated and was patented by Kokichi Mikimoto in 1896. Nacre, an iridescent shell-like substance, coats the natural or man-induced irritant which forms a pearl.

The Cultured Pearl is produced by carefully implanting a small glass bead into the oyster. The perfect glass round is coated with nacre and within approximately 12 months, a cultured pearl of about one millimeter is carefully removed from the oyster. The cultured pearls of Japan find competition in the Majorca Madonna pearls from the Island of Majorca. Each Majorca pearl is individually blown and formed by hand, sorted for uniformity of shape and size, then hand dipped in pearline essence 24 times. There is a drying time of eight to ten hours between each dipping. The pearline essence is made from the Majorca Madonna Pearl manufacturers from their own highly secret formula comprised of Sadu fish scale, lacquer and the saliva of the pearl-producing oyster. This saliva like substance is the nacre which forms natural pearls.

Fresh-water pearls are called "river pearls". Salt-water pearls are primarily mounted in 18-carat gold and in platinum. Fresh-water pearls are set in a lower carat. Pearls are thought of as off-white iridescent colors, but they are found in variations of pink, gray and black. Black pearls are highly prized.

Pearls have never lost favor during any fashion period and they are represented in all colors, sizes and design treatment throughout the 1925-1975 periods. One maxim about jewelry is that "pearls are always in vogue", and a lady is properly attired when her jewelry accessory is "simple pearls". Added to strings of pearls, is the high fashion "look" of many chains, lockets, beads and other prized innovations of fashion jewelry designers. The vogue in 1950-60 was the combination of pearls with *faux* gemstones, particularly turquoise color or lapis.

PEKING GLASS

When it is a light green glass, it is sometimes called "poor man's jade"; however, Peking glass is manufactured in many other shades of glass, imitating the myriad colors of jade. The original Peking glass is a product of China. 1925-1935 was a favored period for jewelry made of this material.

PENDANTS (also see *LAVALIERE* and MEDALLIONS)

In 1910, the vogue for low collars invited all sorts of pretty neck ornaments such as pendants, medallions, *lavalieres* and brooches. The most favored was the pendant, which was often enhanced by a black *moire* ribbon rather than a chain.

The delicate metal work was invariably the cool gray of platinum, the new 20th Century precious ore coming into prolonged use. Many of the beautiful pendants included fine wires twisted into filigree work, and much of the metal had a very thin edge or depth. Enamel work was very popular, and the pendants of the 1925-1940 periods reflect this vogue. Pendants remain in the fashion jewelry domain, with some pendants being detachable from a necklace or heavy linked chain.

PHOENIX

A bird represented by the heron or eagle motif in Egyptian mythology. According to legend, it was consumed by fire but rose from its ashes. Thus, the Phoenix symbolizes resurrection and an emblem of immortality. It also appears in Chinese symbolic motifs. Art Deco designs stylized the heron and eagle and these variations appear on much of the Deco and Moderne jewelry pieces.

PIERCE WORK

Die-cast frame which is cut and engraved with a great deal of open work in the metal.

PIETRA DURA - pyǎ trǎ dōo′ rä - (see MOSAIC)

PIN

Origin of the word is thought to be from the Latin "spina", a thorn found on the Spina Christi tree. Natural thorns are still used as pinning devices in some parts of the world. A pin is a device for attaching or securing many things. It can be strictly functional, decorative or both.

PINS (or Brooches)

Because yesteryear clothing lacked today's modern laundry techniques, collars, frills, ribbons, etc., were detachable. Many of the collars and cuffs, etc., were pinned in place by exquisite "lace pins", most often of delicate filigree or open work.

A small pin, which has long since been forgotten, was the novelty "safety pin", that came in vogue around 1901. These were offered in 10K gold and were sometimes called "negligee collar pins". They resembled a very narrow barrett or bar pin. They were also called "handy pins", sold in pairs in a myriad of designs executed in a choice of gold front, gold filled, sterling silver or black enamel.

The bar pin is usually a one or two inch horizontal pin of gold or silver, with many innovations and variations of the jeweler's art. It was worn at the collar or neckline of a woman's garment, and sometimes used to join a detachable collar to the frock.

Sterling silver brooch pins were most often engraved or had open lacework or filigree work. The *baroque* scroll patterns were the most desirable in Victorian times, but this gave way to *Art Nouveau* designs, and finally the renditions of the Deco and Moderne jewelers.

Cape or jersey pins were two pins attached by a chain. Much in demand during the turn of the century, they drifted out of vogue during the twenties only to be all the rage in the 1930's. Variations on this theme are seen in the "sweater pins" worn in the 1950's-1960's when twin sweater sets were the rage. The matching long-sleeved sweater was fashionably worn over the shoulders, and a sweater-guard pinned each side, drawn by the short chain to keep the sweater from slipping.

There were many types of pinning devices, such as veil pins, cuff pins, stickpins, and "beauty pins", the latter worn in place of studs on women's "shirtwaists" (the name for blouses in America). In France, women's blouses were called *"chemisettes"*. Both "shirtwaists" and "chemisettes" imitated the *Renaissance* sleeve: fullness at the cuff, which was accentuated by cuff buttons.

The main difference between pins and brooches is that pins are first and foremost **utilitarian** and then decorative, whereas brooches are primarily decorative. Today, we refer to all kinds of decorative brooches as either **pins** or **brooches**. If the object is exceptionally large in dimension or laden with gemstones, or of grandiose design, the piece is called a BROOCH.

PIQUE - pe̊-kǎ

Inlaying of gold or silver into genuine tortoise shell, ivory or horn.

PLASTICS (also see BAKELITE and CELLULOID)

Term applied to a group of synthetic chemical products with the distinct quality enabling them to be molded, carved, laminated or pressed into many shapes, sizes and designs. Tortoise, horn, mother-of-pearl, wood, marble, jet and amber were all imitated in plastics.

As with fine French paste, plastic jewelry -- particularly of the Art Deco and Art Moderne periods (1925-1940) -- are not **imitations** of earlier jewelry, but are an art form highly collectible today. Renditions in Bakelite and other fine plastics from 1925-1940, are examples of what exquisite artistry can be accomplished in plastics.

The finest plastic renditions are the 1925-1935 productions; but in 1940 much plastic jewelry was produced due to World War II and shortages of metals.

"The Society of Decorative Plastics", P.O. Box 199, Guerneville, California 95446, publishes a bi-monthly newsletter of great interest to those who favor plastic jewelry. Catherine Yronwode and Dean Mullaney, Editors, will answer queries providing a SASE is enclosed with your letter. **"Collectible Plastics"**, the name of the club's newsletter, issued Vol. 1, No. 2, featuring SPOTLIGHT ON BRACELETS, (December 1984). Any collector of plastic jewelry will be educated by this feature.

Andrea DiNoto's superior publication, **"Art Plastic: Designed for Living"**, is listed in the BIBLIOGRAPHY section of this book, and is a **must read**, long needed, reference about the increasingly collectible: PLASTICS.

PLATINUM

From the Spanish word "platin", meaning silver. Most platinum jewelry came after 1920, with the new discoveries of platinum in Canada and South America.

Platinum is much more expensive than gold due to its rarity. Because it is heavier than gold, it is not often used in very large jewelry pieces. Rhodium and palladium are of the platinum family, but chrome is an alloy which is utilized for a very good, hard, shiny surface. Platinum itself is a more dull silver-color, very rich when set with diamonds or other precious gems. Platinum is still a very rare and expensive commodity.

PLIQUE-A-JOUR - plè-kǎ ǎ jèr´

A translucent *cloisonne* in which there is no metal backing for the enamel work. During firing, a metal supportive base is used until firing ceases. Then, when the piece has cooled and the enamel has hardened, the finished product no longer requires this base so the support is removed.

PROTOTYPE

The original first model to be copied in either the method of casting or molding. A prototype is actually modeled after an original conception of a design or pattern done on the drawing board. Jewelry designers provide renditions on paper, from which a prototype is made for casting or molding a piece for which a die can be produced for mass production. (See CASTING and DIE STAMPING).

PURSES (Bags)

Most collectors may be surprised to learn that frames of mesh bags were works of very fine jewelers. Diamonds and other precious gems were often threaded into the mesh. The jewels were set into precious ores. Some purses were made entirely of seed pearls. Enamelling was extensive and lavish. Frames were rich in *repousse´* work, hand engraving or cutwork. Gemstones were introduced in the clasp or the chain. The bags were made as carefully as a jeweler would make a watch. Many required no less than three months to complete because of the intricate workmanship.

Cut steel beads were very popular and bead bags with conventional floral colors were considered handsome and dressy. The frame usually complemented the tone of the beads used. Beaded purses were much less expensive than metallic mesh purses. Mesh purses demanded the very finest jeweler's art and ingenuity, with its fancy weaves such as the star pattern, zigzag, plaid, daisy pattern, basket weave, herring-bone and even reversible mesh.

At the beginning of the 20th Century, the mesh purse went to the extreme, using pinks and greens, or purples and blue ostrich feathers dyed and then sewn right on to the purses. They were really much more daring and less conservative than the previous mesh and beaded bags in a square shape. The **new** purses of the Deco period were triangular in shape, so that coins would drop dead center into the "point" and not get lost.

"Opera and handkerchief bags" were in vogue beginning in autumn of 1910, and they were reported to be delicately tinted suede embroidered with mock gems. The frames, clasp and chains were usually of gold and silver and were purchased separately. Many of the women's magazines had directions for making the various types of pouches which were then attached to the jeweled frames to complete the purse or bag.

Unless marked "sterling", silver mesh purses were mainly of German silver or gun metal. Silver mesh purses were designed either with a drawstring, a bracelet loop, or with a finely detailed snap-type frame done in high relief or set with imitation stones. Sterling mesh bags were manufactured by Weizenegger Bros., Newark, N.J., while Levitt & Gold, New York, made 14K and platinum mesh bags. Another famous American maker was Whiting-Davis, a company reputed for their gorgeous silver frames. Whiting-Davis is still in business, producing not only purses, but fine chain to the fashion jewelry industry and completed chains to retailers who are proud to sell them with the respected tag: "Whiting-Davis".

Beaded drawstring bags were highly fashionable accessories in the "jazz age" of the "Roarin' Twenties". Many of these beaded drawstrings were imported from France and were of sterling, or gold frames set with precious and ornamental gems.

Beaded bags always keep their beautiful, original color. Most beads are iridescent with high luster, and transparent. Silk thread, being opaque, absorbed the color of the bead, thus the thread and beads were blended. Purple beads were combined with violet thread; light and medium blue beads were strung with gray or other shades of blue thread. Bead makers described their wares as ". . . gold iridescent lusters and transparent iridescent beads. Radiant shades, such as golden brown, jade, green, violet, etc., are blended with tints of translucent gold in the same beads to make truly gorgeous bags . . ."

Any collector of purses and bags can attest to the beauty of these accessories. Many are truly works of art. With cheaper labor in the Orient, beaded and mesh purses and evening bags in particular, are bringing back the vogue dormant since World War II.

REPOUSSE' - rĕ-pōo-să

Decorating metal by pushing out from behind or from the reverse side, in order to create a design in relief. *Repousse'* is work in metal. Working from the front, is called *intaglio*, which can be achieved in metal and/or gem. However, neither process can be done in **glass** or **plastics**, which must be molded. After coming out of the molds, glass can be put against a tin wheel to heighten faceting; plastics can be hand cut or carved.

RHINESTONE (or Brilliants. Also see CRYSTAL)

Rhinestones take their name from the River Rhine, Germany. Rhinestones are quite simply faceted glass, set with a foil backing to give it highlights and brilliance -- hence the term "brilliants". Rhinestones are inferior to Austrian crystal, French paste or the earlier *strass*. (see STRASS). Rhinestones cannot be cleaned successfully. Once the foil is damaged by scratching or emersion into water, the glass loses its brilliance.

At one time, "rhinestones" meant rock crystals taken from the bed of the River Rhine, but actually the resemblance to the tiny rock crystals in the bed of the Rhine River may have led to this deception. Besides foiling, rhinestones may have a painted surface to refract the light. Unlike genuine gems with natural properties of refraction, rhinestones rely entirely on either a high lead content (as in Austrian crystals which require no foiling) or silver, gold or tinted foil to lend them sparkle.

Unlike fine paste jewelry used to make reproductions of crown jewels as protection against robbery, modern rhinestone jewelry fashionable in the early 1930's through the 1960's (with a flamboyant revival in the 1980's), was made for the eager consumer masses seeking a bright spot in a dark depression. "Depression-expression" began following the 1925 rise of Art Deco, and seemed to lead into a bright beginning. The "bright promise" for the weary housewife came with Art Moderne innovations, particularly the "glitz" of rhinestone jewelry appearing first as clips and pins, then the "blitz" of the 1950's-1960's.

RHODIUM

Term normally used when electroplating objects with a platinum alloy.

RIM

The outside edge of a set stone.

RINGS

The "father of jewelry" was Prometheus. According to Pliny, Hercules cut Prometheus loose from the chains which fastened Prometheus to Mount Caucasus. Prometheus supposedly made a ring out of one of the links, bezel-set a portion of the rock against which he had been chained, and created what's considered the first ring and the first "gem".

There's a great deal of sweet romance and legend bound up in the wedding ring. When the first glow of Christianity lighted the world, Pliny the Elder told of a custom his people had borrowed from the ancients of the Nile, that of giving a ring of iron to pledge a betrothal. Such customs from the dim past and the ceremonies which have evolved today, have definitely changed from those early times.

In 1893, Prince Albert presented Queen Victoria with a wedding ring in the form of a serpent. Because of that presentation, and the 1922 opening of King Tut's Tomb, the serpent design is found in many forms of jewelry then and through the Art Deco period and into the late thirties.

In 1900, rings with colored stones were not in vogue for engagement rings. The fashionable engagement ring was a solitaire diamond or smaller stone set in a simple mounting.

"Anti-rheumatic" rings came in just before the turn of the century. They were of gold shell on the outside, with gray metal on the inside.

In 1901, The *Delineator* reported that beautiful rings "proper for a man" would be a solitaire diamond, cat's eye or other precious stone mounted in a gypsy or handsome carved gold setting.

Women did not consider rings their province until the early 18th Century, and then they were mostly "glove rings", worn on the forefinger. Prior to that, most men of nobility wore rings as seals. The period when rings were most commonly worn by both sexes begins from 1875 to the present day.

In the Deco period, several rings were displayed and considered vogue-ish. But during the depression and post WWII, only rings signifying betrothal or marriage were worn by women. By the early 1960's, and to the present time, rings of all sizes and designs are worn singly or in multiples.

"Token rings" were the most desirable gift for the betrothed from 1880 to around 1910. Such a ring, with clasped hands, was called "Mizpah". Translated, "Mizpah" means: "The Lord watch between me and thee when we are absent one from another". These rings were greatly exchanged during World War I, and revived again during World War II.

"Costume" rings of imitation stones and lesser metals were prized during the 1930's, again in the 1950's and again in the 1970's to the present time.

Double-ring ceremonies were initiated during WWII. In the 1940's, it was common practice to present the "girl of my dreams" with a class ring in lieu of a proper engagement ring. Many a war-bride lacked the traditional diamond engagement ring, but in subsequent years of prosperity, a diamond ring was given on a 10th or 20th anniversary -- although tradition has it that the diamond is the jewel for the 60th anniversary. Perhaps the separations of war brought a quickening of needs to make up for lost time, or a realization and urgency to "live today". In any event, self-indulgence and the joy of giving to a loved one made the jewelry industry prosper, grow and soar in popularity. Rings for any occasion prevailed above all else in purchases of jewelry. Grandmother Rings, Birthstone Rings, Valentine Day Rings, Anniversary Rings, Friendship Rings, Souvenir Rings, Betrothal Rings, Class Rings, Initial Rings and just about any other event could be commemorated in rings fashioned with gems, gemstones or imitations and synthetics.

ROCOCO STYLE

An enriched and embellished ornamentation with much profusion of shellwork, scrolls, flowers, figures and an excess of broken, irregular curves framing a major theme of the piece. To work in Rococo style is to add a Baroque (or heavy type of ornamentation) to Rococo.

Rococo ornamentation was revived in the 1930's, departing from the continuous flowing and gentle lines of *Art Nouveau*. Rococo design has always influenced, more or less, fashionable jewelry from one epoch into another. Modern jewelry is no exception.

ROLLED GOLD

A thin leaf of gold used in plating lesser metals. Methods vary from rolling to electroplating a coat of gold over a inferior metal.

ROSE CUT

The faceting of a gem, genuine or imitation, before the turn of the century. The brilliant-cut was not commonly used before 1905, but by 1920 the brilliant-cut faceting of diamonds and other gemstones was superior and did away with the ordinary rose-cut of the earlier era. However, it is by recognizing the differences between a rose cut, or mine-cut diamond and the brilliant cut of the later period, that one can date antique jewelry.

ROUNDELS

Tiny round beads often used as spacers or separators.

SAUTOIR - sŏ twăr´

A term popularized in 1890 to designate a very long, narrow gold link chain with either a pearl, diamond, or polished agate bead introduced at 1″ or 2″ intervals for the length of the chain. In most cases, the *sautoir* fell below the waistline, held in place at the waist by a brooch. The chain was fastened together by a jeweled slide which prevented its separation at the bosom. Other *sautoirs* flaunted tassles which hung 3″ to 6″ longer, requiring the chain to be "tucked in" at the wasitline.

In the first decade of the 20th Century, *sautoirs* were advertised in various jewelry catalogues as long chains with a center drop to accomodate detachable tassles, pendants or other conceits. The term is now considered archaic, though it is sometimes revived and used to describe the extremely long, beaded necklaces of the twenties.

SCARABUS (Scarab)

Form of a beetle, the Egyptian symbol of longevity. Many Deco designs were inspired by this form, especially after the opening of King Tut's Tomb in 1922.

SCARF PINS (also see STICKPINS and TIE PINS)

Scarf pins were made for both ladies and gentlemen as seen in the 1890-1930 catalogues. By 1920, they were already being called "cravat pins" or "tie pins" for men, and "scarf pins" for women.

No distinction was made between male or female styles. Many of the pins had a spiral device which kept them from slipping out. Others had fancy innovations such as small shafts at the heads which would secure them against slippage or loss.

Scarf pins offered no end to diversity of design and were mainly set with gems, gemstones and imitation stones or synthetics.

Advertisements for scarf pins most often read: "set with brilliants", which referred to a glass "diamond" or doublet of a popular gem, such as garnet, opal, ruby, moonstone or turquoise.

"SCATTER" PIN

A term prominently used during 1950-1960, when pairs of small pins were worn together, "scattered" from collar to waist, or even pinned to the hipline of a skirt. Pairs could be matched, or merely complement one another. A trio of "scatter" pins were usually very tiny, intricate in design and carefully set with seed pearls, minute rhinestones and even enamelled.

SETTING (see specific type)

A means of incorporating gems, gemstones (genuine, synthetic or imitation), into metal or other elements, with designs known as: BEZEL, BOX, CHANNEL, CLAW, GYPSY, CROWN, ILLUSION, METAL CUP (for rhinestones), *PAVE´* and TIFFANY.

SHANK

A circle forming a ring, or that portion of a ring which is finally joined to the center or focal point. Also, a pin-shank, the utilitarian part of a brooch, stickpin or hatpin, which is then attached to the ornamental object.

SIGNET

A design in a ring or a fob, often utilized as a seal because of its *intaglio* carving or engraving. The design usually portrays an initial, crest or is symbolic. *Intaglio* work may be either in stone, gem or metal.

SILVER (see STERLING)

SILVER GILT (see *VERMEIL*)

Process of applying a thin coat of gold or yellow lacquer over silver, to produce a rich golden color.

SLEEVE BUTTONS (or Studs)

Sleeve buttons come in pairs and are designed quite differently than cuff **links**. Most sleeve buttons snap; some have a leverback -- a small bar attached by a chain wire. Sometimes the bar and frontpiece of the button match in design, which is likely engraving or scroll-work.

The variety of men's sleeve buttons are endless. Many are engraved with large, very detailed insignias; others had real cameos with *intaglio* designs cut into tiger eye.

Exquisite raised work or *repousse´*, was represented by emblems and intricately raised designs, all beautifully executed in tiger eye, goldstone, lava stone, onyx and hematite. Often set with either a real gem or a polished "brilliant", oxidized metals were foremost in desirability.

SLIDES

French slides were mass produced in gold-filled or gilded metal, *baroque* in design, but depending on raised work and enamelling rather than jewels.

English slides relied heavily on inlay work incorporating pieces of bloodstone, carnelian and onyx. These were wrought in to 9 to 18 karat gold. Others of less artistry were of rolled gold and silver.

American slides braved the brilliance of many ornamental gemstones, set into delicately engraved, tiny slides. Larger slides housed garnets, onyx, cameos, rubies, diamonds and emeralds. Much Etruscan-style intricacy or granular work appears on these.

Slide are found in round, flat, square, oblong, oval, barrel-shape and other metallic improvisations. These were available in low-karat to 18-karat; also, there were gold filled, rolled gold and silver slides. They range in size from ¼″ to 2″, with tubular findings to permit passage of a chain. Other designs allowed chains to pass through two holes on either side of hollow work, cork-filled to prevent slippage.

Slides have been collected and made into bracelets, in vogue during 1950-1960. Fine copies and reproductions of slides have been used in fashionable costume jewelry.

SQUARE CUT STONE

Another design cut for gems and rhinestones.

STERLING

A British term referring to the highest standard of silver, fixed at 925 parts of pure silver to 75 parts copper. The word originated with immigrant Germans who came across the English Channel to England. They settled in a geographic area from which they took the name "Easterlings". Jewelers by trade, these Germans who had resettled in England, were called upon to refine silver for coinage. In 1343, the first two letters were dropped from the word, "Easterling", resulting in the nomenclature -- "STERLING". It denotes the highest purity of silver. All British sterling is hallmarked. (See HALLMARKS).

Sterling silver, besides being coinage and utilized for conventional, familiar pieces of jewelry, was also produced as: veil clasps, ornamentation for elastic garters, ornately executed sash slides and buckles (so favored in 1925-1935 periods), additional trimmings for silk and grosgrain belts, hat marks, folding pocket combs, key rings, umbrella straps, bag or trunk checks, belt buckles, slides, ladies' hatband buckles, armlets (garters), hatpins, and frames for purses and bags. All of these so-called "conceits" were wrought in *Nouveau* and earlier design motifs. Sterling silver was, without doubt, the preferred metal for *Art Nouveau* design in Great Britain, Germany, Bohemia, Scandavia and the United States.

STICKPIN (Tie Pin, Scarf Pin, Ascot Pin, Cravat Pin)

Edwardians made frequent use of jewels in men's neckwear. The popularity of the wide tie introduced beautifully accented stickpins. From approximately 1870 into the 20th Century, men and women of carriage wore stickpins in their hunting stock, scarves or cravats. Many of these pieces were stylized forms of the riding crop, the fox, a horse head or a hunting dog. During the high *Art Nouveau* period, and including the *Art Deco* movement, the jeweler's imagination soared, providing today's collector with innumerable miniature works of art conceived in the ornaments atop the stickpin.

Stickpins are set with pearls, turquoise, diamonds, opals, rubies, amethysts, moonstones, coral and even bezel-set real hard-back beetles. These insects found their counterpart in glass or fine paste, particularly in the early twenties and thirties. (See SCARABUS).

Many prize stickpins have been converted into modern day charms, rings and brooches.

STRASS (sometimes called STRASSER)

Brilliant lead glass perfected by Josef Strass, for whom it is named. It is used in creating artificial gems and gemstones of finest quality, often set without any foiling whatsoever. (Also see FOIL and RHINESTONE).

SWIVEL (or Tongue Clip)

A prong-snap connector, mounted in a movable part, then joined by a hook-ring connected to the ends of watch chains. The watch is snapped and hung in this swivel. The swivel is also utilized on *chatelaines*, on charm bracelets and neck chains.

SWIZZLESTICK

A vanity conceit carried by both men and women before the turn of the century. It is more often carried by a man. The swizzlestick was in demand with the coming of sea-going passenger ships.

The swizzlestick extends into an umbrella of fine wires which are then swirled in a glass of champagne to reduce carbonation. In reducing the bubbles, champagne becomes a white wine, more easily digestible, thus reducing one of the causes of sea-sickness.

It was considered a gentlemanly practice to take a swizzlestick (often worn on a long chain and stored in a pocket) and use the extended swizzle by swishing it in the beverage before offering it to a lady. This not only prevented sea-sickness, but avoided "spotting" a lady's make-up. In yesteryear, heavy loose powdering was all that was available--unlike the solid cake powder manufactured today. In addition, swizzlesticks lessoned the chances of a lady belching in "polite society".

Swizzlesticks are still being manufactured in silver-plate, by Tiffany & Co., the originators. However, this conceit is worn more as a fad or fancy than for honest utilitarian purposes. It does make a good conversation piece.

SYNTHETIC

The term differs from **imitation**. **Synthetic** stones are created by man's intelligent application of the chemicals which **nature** has produced through **natural** means. When referring to synthetic gems or gemstones, we refer to the recent developments of man-made diamonds from pure carbon and the **Chatham** emerald which is a synthetic speeding-up process of obtaining emeralds. In the art of synthesizing, man attempts to **duplicate** nature, whereas in chemical **imitations**, man seeks to merely **imitate** it.

Doublets and triplets are stones consisting of two or more layers of material which are adhered to the top layer of a genuine gem. If one were to remove a doublet, triplet or quadruplet from its setting and look at it from its side, under a magnifying glass, the materials can be seen where they were glued together. Ordinarily, a fine paste or a glass substance is glued to the genuine stone to make the gem appear larger. This process is not considered either **synthetic** or **imitation**. In one word: it is outright **fraud**. Nonetheless, it was an accepted practice for many years, and may even continue to the present day.

A fine example of man's ingenuity for creating a **synthetic** product is the cultured pearl. This is produced by man creating an "unnatural" irritation within the oyster's shell. Technically, a cultured pearl could be called synthetic, but since it is not "manufactured" by man, but is rather produced by the workings of nature, it is called **cultured**.

With man harnessing the atom, and with more understanding of the workings and configurations of atoms, it is not too unrealistic or too far reaching to suppose that some day in the not too distant future, many if not all gems will be synthetically produced in competition with the **natural** gem.

TEMPLATE (or Templet)

To make a permanent record or copy of a pattern or design, usually on a thin plate or board which can then be traced or reproduced in a given medium.

TEMPLERS

Jewelry worn by women on the forehead or at the temples, as was in vogue during the 1925 *Art Deco* period. The Arts and Crafts movement revived the ancient popularity of templers and it continued through the *Art Nouveau* period and into the Deco era. Only the modifications in design changed from one period to the other.

TIARA - ti-är-a

The word is derived from a Royal Persian headdress, but is now accepted as any decorative jeweled or flowered headband or semi-circle worn by women for formal wear. The difference between a *tiara* and diadem or crown, is that the latter is worn as a symbol of regal power or a crown of dignity.

TIE PIN (see STICKPIN)

The term is synonymous with stickpin until about 1900. Then the tie pin or cravat pin was called a "tie holder". It resembled a baby's bib clip, except that the tie pin was larger and more ornate. The clasp worked similarly to that of the bib holder. The tie clasps or holders -- a term used interchangably-- were made in all metals, many with raised polished edges, finished in gray, Roman gold, satin, rose and other gold colors. They were engraved, had bright bevelled edges and were also finished in colored enamels in endless varities.

TOPAZ

A gemstone with the characteristic color of yellow which varies from canary to deep orange. In its natural form, it consists of translucent or opaque masses. Topaz is also found in transparent prismatic crystals of white, greenish or bluish colors. These are uncommon. When some topaz is heated, it becomes pink or red. A yellow variety of quartz, namely citrine, is sometimes called "false topaz". Both topaz and citrine were beautifully adapted into Art Deco and Art Moderne period jewelry and remained ever popular through 1950-1975.

TORTOISE-SHELL (or Tortoiseshell)

A yellowish-brown grained substance which is the hard-plate shell from the back of the tortoise. Now an endangered species, the material can no longer be used in the making of decorative objects, including jewelry. Imitation tortoise-shell was manufactured from plastic, and is still imitated in the newer compositions of soft and hard plastics. Sadler Bros. (South Attleboro, Mass.) made imitation **Tortoisene**, used primarily for combs, hair ornaments and fine jewelry. Natural tortoise-shell was also used for these purposes and tortoise *pique* work is highly sought after by collectors. (See *PIQUE* and **PLASTICS**).

TRADEMARKS (see HALLMARKS)

TREMBLER (or Tremblant) See NODDER.

183

TRIANGULAR CUT

A cut for gems and gemstones in a three-pronged or triangular shape. A popular cut for rhinestones.

VERMEIL - vûr′ mil or vûr mǎy

Silver, bronze or copper that has been gilded. Also a red (vermillion color) varnish applied to a gilded surface to give high luster. Ordinarily, one thinks of *vermeil* as a gold wash over sterling silver. (see **GILT** or **GILDED**).

VERMICELLI - vûr-mi-sel′-i

The word in Italian means, "little worms". This aptly describes the thin gold wire which is twisted in a decorative design resembling squirming worms. **Vermicelli** should not be confused with granular work. (See **GRANULAR**).

VICTORIAN ERA (1837-1901)

The 64-year reign of Queen Victoria, during which came vast political and social changes, a rapid growth of industrialization, but a retention of strict moral rules and decorum challenged during the last half of her reign.

"Victorian" now implies a "straight-laced, old fashioned" approach to both morals and standards. However, the Victorian Era was, in fact, a time of great change from the Dark Ages to an Age of Enlightenment. The period is important to those interested in jewelry as a whole, because much of the inspiration for design was either represented or newly discovered during this epoch.

VINAIGRETTE - vĭn-à-grĕt′

A small conceit usually executed in gold or silver, with perforations on top. It held aromatic vinegar, smelling salts or spirits of amonia. This was a "necessary" carried by expectant mothers, from the turn of the century through the 1940's.

WAX-BEAD PEARLS (also see **PEARLS**)

Man-made pearls from the Bohemian area and Murano, Italy. They were shipped by the ton to fashionable Paris and London and utilized in hair and dress decorations and jewelry. Later, these imitation pearls were used in American mass-produced jewelry, even to the present day. The imitation pearls have a bead base, covered by a wax luster or by iridescent glass. These pearls have a tendency to yellow with age and/or peel.

WATCHES and WRIST WATCHES

There are many books on the subject and the reader is urged to research them. The reader should also venture into the many old catalogues which provide enlarged drawings and engravings of the innerworks of watch movements as well as the outer decorative cases, including hunting cases, "pie-crust" cases and simple bezeled cases.

A summary appears in the GLOSSARY section of the author's book, *100 Years of Collectible Jewelry: 1850-1950*, now in its 5th printing (Collector Books, 1978). Revised and updated pricing appears in the later editions, including 1985 printing.

Up until WWI, the pocket watch and the decorative lapel watch were fashionable. But with the wearing of military uniforms and with women doing factory work requiring untypical clothing as worn in the past, both sexes adopted the wrist watch, first initiated in the British army.

From 1920-1930 there were very stylish Art Deco flat, evening watches for men, worn with evening dress and without a chain. Some of the flat watches for men held a combination cigar cutter. Art Deco watches, in sterling or platinum, set with marcasites in silver, and diamonds in platinum, were prized by women during this same period.

ZIRCON

A transparent variety of crystals which come in many colors such as yellow, brown, red, pink, etc. It is often used in birthstone rings as alternates to precious gems or ornamental gemstones. The crystals are actually a transparent gemstone, not to be confused with man-made glass or paste.

ZIRCON-CUT

Similar to faceted rose-cut diamonds.

Section VI

Unit I
Bibliography - References - Recommended Reading

Unit II
Credits and Ackowledgements

Unit I
Bibliography

Books

BAKER, LILLIAN, *Art Nouveau & Art Deco Jewelry*, Collector Books, Paducah, Kentucky (1981)

_____, *Hatpins and Hatpin Holders: An Illustrated Value Guide*, Collector Books, Paducah, Kentucky (1983) Supplemental work to the 1976 Encyclopedia.

_____, *100 Years of Collectible Jewelry: 1850-1950*, Collector Books, Paducah, Kentucky (First printing, 1976; Revised 1978, 1983 and 1985)

_____, *The Collector's Encyclopedia of Hatpins and Hatpin Holders*, Collector Books, Paducah, Kentucky. (Out of print, but available at most research libraries and museums with costume departments.)

BAUER, DR. JAROSLAV, *Minerals, Rocks and Precious Stones*, Octopus Books Limited, London. (1974)

BURGESS, F.W., *Antique Jewelry & Trinkets*, Tudor Publishing Co., New York (1962)

DARLING, ADA W., *The Jeweled Trail*, Wallace-Holmstead Book Co., Des Moines, Iowa (1971)

DiNOTO, ANDREA, *Art Plastic -- Designed for Living*, Abbeville Press, Inc., New York (1984) Cross River Press, Ltd.

FRANCIS, PETER, JR., *The World of Beads Monograph Series, 1 thru 5*, Lapis Route Books, Lake Placid, New York (1979-1982)

DOLAN, MARYANNE, *Collecting Rhinestone Jewelry*, Books Americana, Inc., Florence, Alabama 35630 (1984)

FREGNAC, CLAUDE, *Jewelry from the Renaissance to Art Nouveau*, G.P. Putnam's Sons, New York (1965)

GARSIDE, ANNE, Editor, *Jewelry--Ancient to Modern*, (Walters Art Gallery), The Viking Press, New York (1980)

HASLAM, MALCOLM, *Marks and Monograms of the Modern Movement, 1875-1930*, Charles Scribner's Sons (1977)

HILLIER, BEVIS, *Art Deco of the 20s and 30s*, Studio Vista/Dutton, New York (1968)

HORNUNG, CLARENCE P., *A Source Book of Antiques and Jewelry Designs*, George Braziller, New York (1963)

HUGHES, GRAHAM, *Jewelry*, E.P. Dutton & Co., New York (1966)

_____, *Modern Jewelry*, Crown Publishers, Inc., New York (1963)

_____, *The Art of Jewelry*, The Viking Press, New York (1972)

KENNETT, FRANCIS, *The Collector's Book of Fashions*, Crown Publishers, Inc., New York (1983)

KOCH, ROBERT, *Louis C. Tiffany, Rebel in Glass*, Crown Publishers, Inc., New York (1964)

LESIEUTRE, ALAIN, *The Spirit and Splendor of Art Deco*, Paddington Press, Ltd., New York (1974)

MENTEN, THEODORE, *The Art Deco Style*, Dover Publications, Inc., New York (1972)

MEYER, FRANZ SALES, *The Handbook of Ornament*, Wilcox & Follett Co., New York (1945)

NEWBLE, BRIAN, *Practical Enameling and Jewelry Work*, The Viking Press, New York (1967)

ROSE, AUGUSTUS F. and ANTONIO CIRINO, *Jewelry Making and Design*, Dover Publications, Inc., New York (1967)

SJOBERG, JAN and OVE, *Working with Copper, Silver and Enamel*, Van Nostrand Reinhold Co., New York (1974)

Articles

BAKER, STANLEY L., "Collecting Art Deco", *The Antique Trader*, Dubuque, Iowa (Dec. 10, 1974)

BUCK, J.H., *Historical Sketch of Maker's Marks and Early American Legislation as to Silver*, The Jewelers' Circular Publishing Co., New York (1886)

DiNOTO, ANDREA, "Bakelite Envy", *Connoisseur Magazine*, The Hearst Corporation, New York (July 1985)

DOERFER, JANE, *MassBay Antiques*, Vol. 3, No. 6, "Costume Jewelry: High Style at Low Cost", (Sept. 1982)

GORDON, ELEANOR & JEAN NERENBORG, "Early Plastic Jewelry", *The Antique Trader*, Dubuque, Iowa (Nov. 26, 1974)

REDD, LISA, "Puttin' on the Glitz", *Money Magazine*, (October 1984)

Magazines

Flair, Cowles Magazines, Inc., New York (April 1950)

Harper's Bazaar, Dec. 1945, Oct. 1967, Dec. 1968, fashion plates.

Ladies' Home Journal, June 1916, Sept. 1931, fashion plates and ads

Modern Jewelry, Hurst House Inc., Kansas City, MO (Mar. 1977)

Ornament, Ornament, Inc., Los Angeles, Calif. (Vol. 6, No. 1, 1982)

Vogue Magazine, April 1965, Sept. 1966, Nov. 1966, Sept. 1967, fashion plates.

Periodicals and Catalogues

Collectible Plastics, Vol. 1, No. 2, Dec. 1984-Jan. 1985. *The Society of Decorative Plastics,* P.O. Box 199, Guerneville, California 95446

Eisenberg Ice, Fall 1969, Spring 1970. Eisenberg Jewelry, 22 West Madison St., Chicago, Illinois 60602

Art Deco Catalog, Oct. 14-Nov. 30, 1970, Finch College Museum of Art, New York

Fine Antique & Modern Jewelry Auction, January 22, 1985, Phillips Fine Art Auctioneers & Appraisers, 406 E. 79th St., New York 10021

Schroeder's Insider & Price Update, Monthly Newsletter published for the antique and collectible marketplace, August 1983 - September 1985, Jean Cole, Editor. Schroeder Publishing Co., Inc., 5801 Kentucky Dam Road, Paducah, Kentucky 42001.

International Club for Collectors of Hatpins & Hatpin Holders, (Founded August 1977), Monthly Newsletter, *Points*; Semi-Annual *Pictorial Journal*. Information: Send SASE to ICCofH&HH, 15237 Chanera Avenue, Gardena, California 90249. Founder & Editor: Lillian Baker.

Jablonec Costume Jewelry--An Historic Outline, Stanislav Urban & Zuzana Pestova, Museum of Glassware & Costume Jewelry, Jablonec, Orbis, Prague, Czech.

The Bead Journal, Winter 1976, Spring 1976 editions. P.O. Box 24C47, Los Angeles, California 90024. Editor, Robert K. Liu, Ph.D.

The International Silver & Jewlery Fair & Seminar, 1985, The Dorchester, Park Lane, London WI, England (January 31, 1985)

The Sophisticate, Winter 1984/85. *The Art Deco Society of California*, 109 Minna Street, Suite 339, San Francisco, California 94105

Trade-Marks of the Jewelry & Kindred Trades, The Jewelers' Circular Publishing Co., 11 John St., New York (1915)

NOTE: Further references and recommended reading can be found in the *Bibliographies* published in Lillian Baker's books listed herein. Although some titles in these listings are out-of-print, they are usually available through reference libraries.

Unit II

Credits & Acknowledgements

The author expresses her deep gratitude for the kindness, courtesy, interest and assistance of all those whose names appear in various sections of this publication. Individual, much deserved praise, would require a full volume.

Sincere thanks to all those who either supplied photographs or the actual jewelry to be photographed for the color and black and white pictures which provide such an eye-appealing addition to this book.

Special acknowledgement is given to all the photographers and illustrators credited with their excellent work. I would be remiss if I did not once again express additional praise to my friends, Dave and Barbara Lee Hammell -- and particularly to Dave Hammell -- for their patience and cooperation while the author worked on the layouts of the hundreds of pieces of jewelry. Dave's exceptional talent shows in the color photographs appearing on the cover and the plates herein. It has been a pleasure working with the Hammell team in the past, on this book project, and I am in anticipation of future assignments as co-workers.

Heartfelt thanks to those who dug into their archives and their "instant recall", to provide research and background materials so essential to an encyclopedic work.

Credit must be given to Lucile Nisen, who quietly and uncomplainingly assisted me in the tedious clerical work necessary to compile extensive cross-index references contained in this book. Despite the pressures and demands of the author, she continued to work at "beck and call" of an author who, I confess, can sometimes be a hard taskmaster.

Kudos to Bill and Meredith Schroeder, my publishers, and to their wonderful, cooperative Editor, Steve Quertermous and Staff at COLLECTOR BOOKS, for their efforts and continued confidence in my work.

Many thanks to the scores of persons, archivists, company representatives, far and wide, whose correspondence and contacts aided greatly in formulating a cohesive representation of the jewelry fashion industry.

Credit and acknowledgement to my husband is expressed in the DEDICATION of my book. To this I add love and affection to him and to my family.

Lillian Baker
Alondra Park, Gardena, CA 90249

Section VII

Unit I
An Addendum

Unit II
Value Guide

Unit I
An Addendum

Collectible High Fashion Jewelry names, (1925-1975) not represented on plates in this book:

Florenza	Primavera
Judith McCann	Scaasi
Krementz	Whiting & Davis
Oscar De La Renta	

And a special report . . .

Henri Bendel, top fashion establishment, New York, is reported to have been the major purchaser at the January 1985 first-ever auction of high fashion jewelry. Ms. Joyce Jonas, former Head of Jewelry Dept., Phillips -- the auction house and appraisers, whose firm was founded in London in 1796 -- reported to the author via a letter, that the "feed-back from this sale was remarkable, ranging from accolades for having the 'guts' to undertake the auction and legitimize a hitherto neglected and under-appreciated form of jewelry . . ."

Lita Solis-Cohen wrote a series of syndicated columns about this new and exciting type of auction: "Rhinestone Glitter by the Bagfull" and "Costume Jewelry Dazzles Collectors". A Phillips' catalogue and results of the auction are aides to the collector of fashionable collection jewelry. The catalogue is listed in the BIBLIOGRAPHY.

The author believes that any reader of this book will no longer "neglect" nor "under-appreciate" high fashion costume jewelry produced in those truly spectacular show-case years of 1925-1975.

Many of the "name jewelry" in this publication are still in production, with ever increasing diversity. Others have retired from the industry. Joining the "oldtimers" as collectible jewelry of the future, are the serious designer pieces featured in today's high-fashion catalogues or in the spotlight ads of major department stores. The stores, by and large, are the same trend-setters who gave the exciting "showings" of new high fashion jewelry of the past.

There are designers of the 1980's with much promise. Let us trust that such designers of the future, and their producers, will keep careful and complete records plus photographs of the upcoming genre of jewelry which can be added to the important reference works about ornamental high fashion pieces -- past, present and future.

Unit II
Value Guide

Plate 1
Top, left	Brooch	325.00-375.00
Top, right	Earrings	65.00-85.00
Middle	Necklace	250.00-275.00
Center, top	Brooch	45.00-55.00
Bottom, center	Pin	25.00-35.00

Plate 2
Top, row	Pin	15.00-20.00
Row 2	Set: Pin & Earrings	25.00-30.00
Center	Set: Pendant & Earrings	25.00-35.00
Bottom Row	Set: Brooch & Earrings	25.00-30.00

Plate 3
Left	Bracelet	45.00-55.00
Right	Pendant	150.00-175.00
Center, left	Pendant	75.00-85.00
Center, right	Brooch	25.00-35.00
Center	Brooch	65.00-85.00
Bottom, center	Brooch	75.00-85.00
Bottom	Set: Bracelets	40.00-65.00

Plate 4
Left	Cross, w/adjustable 24″ chain	20.00-30.00
Top, center	Set: Pin & Earrings	25.00-30.00
Center	Set: Brooch & Earrings	15.00-20.00
Center, bottom	Award Pin & Medallion, each	10.00
Top, right	Bracelet (Complete set: $55.00-65.00)	10.00
Bottom, right	Cross (with chain, $25.00-35.00)	15.00-20.00

Plate 5
Top	Earrings	10.00-15.00
Center & Bottom	*Parure:* Necklace, earrings & bracelet (set)	85.00-125.00

Plate 6
Row 1, L-R	Set: Pin & Earrings	35.00-45.00
Row 2, L-R	Set: Pin & Earrings	45.00-65.00
Row 3, L-R	Set: Pin & Earrings	45.00-65.00
Bottom, left	Pin	20.00-25.00
Bottom, right	Pin	35.00-45.00

Plate 7
Top	Pin	175.00-225.00
Row 2, L-R	Set: Ring & Earrings	285.00-325.00
Center	Bow Pin w/Locket	225.00-275.00
Row 3	Earrings	65.00-85.00
Row 4	Cameo Brooch	375.00-450.00
Bottom	Earrings	75.00-95.00

Plate 8
Left	Chain	5.00-10.00
Center & top right	*Parure:* Bracelet, Earrings & Brooch (set w/chain)	125.00-145.00
Bottom, right	Set: Pin & Earrings	55.00-65.00

Plate 9
Top Row, L-R	Pin	20.00-30.00
Top Row, L-R	Pin	35.00-45.00
Top Row, L-R	Pin	55.00-65.00
Row 2, L-R	Pin	35.00-45.00
Row 2, L-R	Pin	55.00-65.00
Row 2, L-R	Pin	15.00-20.00
Row 3, L-R	Pin	55.00-65.00
Row 3, L-R	Pin	15.00-20.00
Row 3, L-R	Pin	25.00-35.00
Bottom	Pin	10.00-15.00

Plate 10
Left & Top	Set: Earrings & Bracelet	25.00-35.00
Center & Right, Top to Bottom	*Parure:* Bracelet, Earrings & Brooch (set)	95.00-125.00

Plate 11
Top Row	Set: Brooch w/dangle or button type clip earrings	
	Brooch	35.00-45.00
	Either pair of Earrings	10.00-45.00
Center	Set: Brooch & Earrings	65.00-75.00
Bottom, L-R	Pin	10.00-15.00
Bottom, L-R	Pin only	15.00-20.00
Bottom, L-R	Pin	15.00-25.00

Plate 12
Top	Pin	35.00-55.00
Center	Necklace	110.00-135.00
Center	Brooch	75.00-95.00
Bottom, Left	Set: Pin & Earrings	45.00-65.00
Bottom	Pin	25.00-35.00

Plate 13
Row 1, L-R	Earrings	55.00-65.00
Row 1, L-R	Pin	75.00-85.00
Row 1, L-R	Earrings	45.00-65.00
Row 2, Left	Fur Clip	65.00-85.00
Row 2, Right	Pin	35.00-45.00
Row 3, Center	Pin	85.00-125.00
Row 4	Beads	95.00-135.00

Plate 14
Top, Left	Pin	45.00-55.00
Bottom, Left	Hair Barrett	5.00-10.00
Center	Bracelet	25.00-35.00
Top, Right	Brooch	25.00-35.00
Bottom, Right	Brooch	65.00-85.00

Plate 15
Top	Brooch	35.00-45.00
Center	Bracelet	65.00-95.00
Bottom	Set: Earrings & Necklace	150.00-185.00

Plate 16
Top Row	Earrings	25.00-35.00
Row 2, L-R	Pin	25.00-35.00
Row 2, L-R	Pin	65.00-75.00
Row 2, L-R	Pin	35.00-45.00
Row 3	Bracelet	95.00-125.00
Row 4 & 5	*Parure:* Necklace, Earrings & Bracelet (set)	125.00-145.00

Plate 17
Top, Left	Pin	55.00-75.00
Bottom, Left	Pin	45.00-55.00
Top Center	Brooch	95.00-110.00
Center & Right	Set: Pendant & Earrings	275.00-350.00
Top, Right	Earrings	20.00-30.00
Bottom, Right	Earrings	20.00-30.00

Plate 18
Top Row, Left	Pin	25.00-30.00
Top Row, Right	Ring	25.00-30.00
Center & Bottom	*Parure:* Earrings, Necklace & Bracelet (set)	85.00-125.00

Plate 19
Top, L-R	Set: Brooch w/earrings	110.00-135.00
Center	Pin	85.00-95.00
Bottom	"Dog Collar" necklace	125.00-135.00

Plate 20
Full Plate	Set: Earrings & Necklace	145.00-175.00

Plate 21
Row 1, Left	Earrings	75.00-95.00
Row 1, Right	Dress Clip	95.00-125.00
Row 2	Earrings	175.00-225.00
Row 3	Bracelet	85.00-110.00
Bottom, Left	Earrings	65.00-85.00
Bottom, Right	Earrings	45.00-55.00

Plate 22
Top Row	Bracelet	125.00-145.00
Row 2	Bracelet	95.00-110.00
Row 3	Set: Brooch & Earrings	135.00-150.00
Row 4	Necklace	85.00-110.00
Row 4, Center	Set: Earrings & Pin	95.00-110.00
Bottom	Bracelet	110.00-125.00

Plate 23
Top	Set: Earrings & Pendant-Necklace	85.00-110.00
Row 2, Left	Brooch	65.00-75.00
Row 2, Right	Brooch	65.00-75.00
Bottom	*Parure:* Earrings, Necklace & Bracelet	110.00-125.00

Plate 24
Top, Left	Pin	65.00-95.00
Top, Right	Pin	95.00-125.00
Center	Beads	75.00-95.00
Center	Pin	35.00-45.00
Bottom, Left	Pin	35.00-45.00
Bottom, Right	Pin	40.00-60.00

Plate 25
Top, Right	Pin	45.00-65.00
Center	Brooch	65.00-85.00
Top Left, Center & Bottom	*Parure:* Earrings, Bracelet & Necklace	250.00-325.00

Plate 26
Top	Pin	25.00-35.00
Top, Left	Fur Clip	110.00-125.00
Top, Right	Earrings	35.00-45.00
Center	Brooch	125.00-135.00
Bottom Center, L-R	Set: Brooch & Earrings	65.00-85.00
Bottom, Left	Earrings (clip)	20.00-30.00
Bottom, Right	Fur Clip	75.00-95.00

Plate 27A
Top to Bottom	Necklace	175.00-225.00

Plate 28
Top, Left	Pin	135.00-150.00
Top, Right	Earrings	10.00-15.00
Center, Top	Brooch	35.00-45.00
Bottom, Center	Pendant	75.00-95.00
Bottom	Chain	45.00-55.00

Plate 29
Top, Left	Pin	65.00-85.00
Top, Right	Scarf Pin	95.00-110.00
Row 2, L-R	Earrings	75.00-85.00
Row 2, L-R	Earrings	75.00-95.00
Row 2, L-R	Earrings	95.00-110.00
Row 3, L-R	Pin	85.00-100.00
Row 3, L-R	Earrings	85.00-125.00
Row 3, L-R	Pin	85.00-100.00
Row 4, L-R	Scarf Pin	65.00-75.00
Row 4, L-R	Fur Clip	185.00-225.00
Row 4, L-R	Pin	85.00-95.00

Plate 30
Top Row	Earrings	55.00-65.00
Row 2, Left	Brooch	95.00-110.00
Row 2, Center	Brooch	110.00-145.00
Row 2, Right	Brooch	85.00-95.00
Row 3	Bracelet	95.00-110.00
Row 4, Left	Brooch	85.00-110.00
Row 4, Right	Brooch	55.00-65.00
Bottom Row	Earrings	65.00-85.00

Plate 31
Top	Set: Earrings & Pendant-Necklace	110.00-125.00
Center	Pendant	65.00-75.00
Bottom	Necklace	85.00-95.00

Plate 32
Top, Left	Earrings	20.00-30.00
Top, Right	Earrings	25.00-35.00
Row 2	Bracelet	50.00-65.00
Center	Earrings	20.00-30.00
Bottom	Necklace (w/bracelet, $350.00-375.00 set)	225.00-275.00

Plate 33
Top, L-R	Pin	95.00-135.00
Top, L-R	Earrings	15.00-20.00
Top, L-R	Pin	85.00-95.00
Row 2, L-R & Bottom Row	Set: Earrings & Bracelet	250.00-285.00
Row 2, L-R & Bottom Row	Set: Earrings & Bracelet	125.00-145.00
Row 2, L-R & Bottom Row	Set: Earrings & Bracelet	110.00-135.00

Plate 34
Top	*Parure:* Set: Earrings, Brooch & Bracelet	125.00-135.00
Center	Necklace	65.00-85.00
Center	Earrings	15.00-20.00
Bottom, Left	Brooch	35.00-45.00
Bottom, Right	Pin	25.00-30.00

Plate 35
Top	Pin	75.00-95.00
Center	Earrings	45.00-65.00
Center to Bottom	Necklace	150.00-175.00

Plate 36
Row 1, Left	Pin	20.00-25.00
Row 1, Right	Earrings	55.00-65.00
Row 2	Bracelet	125.00-135.00
Row 3	Bracelet	165.00-185.00
Row 4, Left	Pair: Dress Clips	35.00-45.00
Row 4, Right	Brooch	65.00-85.00
Row 5	Bracelet	75.00-95.00
Row 6, Left	Earrings	25.00-35.00
Row 6, Right	Set: Pin & Earrings	45.00-65.00

Plate 37
Top, L-R	Scarf Pin	15.00-25.00
Top, L-R	Earrings	65.00-75.00
Top, L-R	Pin	95.00-100.00
Top, L-R	Fur Clip	125.00-145.00
Center	Brooch	325.00-375.00
Bottom, Left	Earrings	65.00-75.00
Bottom, Center	Pendant-Necklace	250.00-285.00
Bottom, Right	Pin	35.00-45.00

Plate 38
Top, Left	Earrings	55.00-65.00
Top, Right	Pin	45.00-55.00
Center	Earrings	10.00-15.00
Center	Necklace	35.00-45.00
Bottom, Left	Brooch	95.00-110.00
Bottom, Right	Scarf Pin	25.00-35.00

Plate 39
Row 1	Earrings	45.00-55.00
Row 2	Bracelet	65.00-85.00
Center	Brooch	75.00-85.00
Bottom	Necklace	150.00-175.00

Plate 40
Top, Left	Brooch	45.00-65.00
Top, Right	Pin	25.00-35.00
Center Row, Left	Pin	25.00-35.00
Center Row, Middle	Compact	250.00-300.00
Center Row, Right	Pin	10.00-15.00
Bottom, Left	Earrings	10.00-15.00
Bottom, Right	Pin	10.00-15.00

Plate 41
Top, Left	Pin	55.00-65.00
Top, Right	Brooch	65.00-75.00
Center, Left	Compact	250.00-300.00
Center, Right	Set: Pin & Earrings	75.00-95.00
Bottom, Left	Pin	45.00-65.00
Bottom, Right	Bracelet	65.00-85.00

Plate 42
Top, L-R	Pin	25.00-35.00
Top, L-R	Pin	35.00-45.00
Top, L-R	Pin	25.00-35.00
Row 2, L-R	Pin	35.00-45.00
Row 2, L-R	Earrings	25.00-35.00
Row 2, L-R	Pin [$35.00-45.00 w/earrings]	20.00-25.00
Row 3, L-R	Earrings	25.00-35.00
Row 3, L-R	Pin	45.00-65.00
Row 3, L-R	Earrings	20.00-30.00
Row 4, L-R	Pin	15.00-20.00
Row 4, L-R	Pin	20.00-35.00
Row 4, L-R	Kilt Pin	15.00-20.00

Plate 43
Top Left & Center	Set: Earrings & Necklace	45.00-55.00
Top Center	Pin	20.00-30.00
Top, Right	Pin	25.00-35.00
Center	Brooch	45.00-65.00
Bottom	Set: Bracelet & Earrings	25.00-35.00

Plate 44
Top, Left	Set: Necklace & Drop Earrings	135.00-165.00
Top, Right	Pin	65.00-85.00
Center & Bottom	Set: Bracelet & Necklace	275.00-325.00
Bottom, Center	Pin	55.00-75.00

Plate 45
Top	Pin	75.00-95.00
Left	Bracelet	45.00-55.00
Row 2, L-R	Pin	35.00-45.00
Row 2, L-R	Pin	85.00-95.00
Row 3, L-R	Pin	45.00-55.00
Row 3, L-R	Pin	45.00-55.00
Bottom	Pin	55.00-65.00

Plate 46
Top, L-R	Pin	75.00-95.00
Top, L-R	Brooch	85.00-110.00
Top, L-R	Pin	85.00-110.00
Row 2	Bracelet	55.00-65.00
Row 3, L-R	Pin	110.00-145.00
Row 3, L-R	Pin	65.00-85.00
Row 3, L-R	Pin	125.00-165.00
Row 4, L-R	Pendant	25.00-35.00
Row 4, L-R	Pendant	35.00-45.00
Row 4, L-R	Pin	25.00-35.00

Plate 47
Top, L-R	Pin	20.00-30.00
Top, L-R	Pin	65.00-85.00
Top, L-R	Pin	25.00-35.00
Row 2, L-R	Pin	25.00-35.00
Row 2, L-R	Brooch	35.00-40.00
Row 2, L-R	Pin	10.00-15.00
Row 3, L-R	Pin	10.00-15.00
Row 3, L-R	Pin	65.00-85.00
Row 3, L-R	Pin	15.00-25.00
Bottom, L-R	Pin	35.00-45.00
Bottom, L-R	Pin	45.00-65.00
Bottom, L-R	Pin	25.00-35.00

Plate 48

Top, Left	Set: Pin and Earrings	125.00-150.00
Top, Right	Pin	45.00-65.00
Row 2, Left	Pin	55.00-75.00
Row 2, Right	Set: Earrings & Pin	75.00-95.00
Row 3	Set: Earrings & Pin	125.00-150.00
Row 4, L-R	Pin	45.00-55.00
Row 4, L-R	Pin	45.00-55.00
Row 4, L-R	Pin	45.00-55.00

Plate 49

Top, Center	Pin	85.00-95.00
Top, Left & Right	Scarf Pins, each	55.00-75.00
Center	Brooch	95.00-110.00
Bottom	Set: Necklace & Earrings	95.00-125.00

Plate 50

Top, L-R	Pin	25.00-35.00
Top, L-R	Pin	125.00-150.00
Top, L-R	Pin	125.00-150.00
Row 2, L-R	Earrings	55.00-65.00
Row 2, L-R	Set: Pin & Earrings	125.00-145.00
Row 2, L-R	Earrings	55.00-65.00
Row 3 & 4	Set: Bracelet & Earrings	275.00-325.00

Plate 51

Left to Right	Bracelet [w/pendant & earrings $110.00-125.00]	25.00-35.00
Left to Right	Bracelet [complete set $135.00-150.00]	55.00-65.00
Left to Right	Bracelet	15.00-25.00
Left to Right	Bracelet [complete set $95.00-110.00]	20.00-25.00
Top, Right	Pin	15.00-20.00
Bottom, Right	Pin	25.00-35.00

Plate 52

Top	Pin	45.00-55.00
Center	Earrings	75.00-85.00
Center	Buckle or Scarf Pin	35.00-45.00
Center	Necklace or Choker	45.00-65.00
Bottom	Bracelet	45.00-55.00
Bottom	Brooch	55.00-65.00

Plate 53

Top, Left	Pin	15.00-25.00
Top, Right	Earrings	45.00-55.00
Center	Earrings	55.00-65.00
Center	Beaded Necklace	65.00-95.00
Bottom, Left	Earrings	35.00-45.00
Bottom, Right	Earrings	45.00-55.00

Plate 54

Top	Bracelet	25.00-35.00
Center	Pin	35.00-45.00
Bottom	Set: Earrings & Necklace	135.00-145.00

Plate 55

Top, L-R	Pin	25.00-35.00
Top, L-R	Earrings	55.00-65.00
Top, L-R	Pin	45.00-65.00
Center	Pin	45.00-55.00
Center	Necklace	55.00-75.00
Bottom, L-R	Fur Clip	95.00-110.00
Bottom, L-R	Earrings	25.00-35.00
Bottom, L-R	Pin	35.00-45.00

Black and White Photographs

Plate B-1

Top	Set: Earrings & Necklace	145.00-185.00
Bottom, Center	Pin	75.00-85.00
Bottom	Necklace	175.00-225.00

Plate B-2

Top, Left	Pin	65.00-75.00
Top, Right	Pin	75.00-95.00
Center	Pin	65.00-85.00
Bottom, Center	Pin	75.00-95.00
Bottom	Necklace	175.00-225.00

Plate B-3

Top Row, L-R	Pin	85.00-95.00
Top Row, L-R	Earrings	55.00-75.00
Top Row, L-R	Pin	85.00-95.00
Row 2	Set: Pin & Earrings	85.00-95.00
Row 3, Left	Pin	75.00-85.00
Row 3, Right	Pin	65.00-85.00
Bottom	Set: Earrings & Necklace	175.00-225.00

Plate B-4

Left, Top to Bottom	Scarf Pin	65.00-75.00
Left, Top to Bottom	Pin	55.00-65.00
Left, Top to Bottom	Pin	45.00-55.00
Left, Top to Bottom	Pin	45.00-55.00
Right	Bracelet	95.00-110.00

Plate B-5

Top	Set: Earrings & Necklace	125.00-135.00
Bottom	*Parure:* Ring, pendant-necklace and pendant-earrings (set)	250.00-325.00

Plate B-6

Top	Hair Ornament	55.00-75.00
Center	Pair: Side Combs	65.00-85.00
Bottom	Pin	55.00-65.00

Plate B-7

Full Plate	Set: Earrings & Necklace	150.00-175.00

Plate B-8

Full Plate	Choker	35.00-45.00

Plate B-9

Full Plate	Brooch	85.00-110.00

[Plates B-10 through B-22, no values given for pieces featured in advertisements or in other publications. Only jewelry which the author has had IN HAND has been given a guide as to retail market values. Please see notation regarding values printed in this publication, at the front of the book.]

Plate B-23

Full Plate	Set: Cuff Links & Tie-Tac	75.00-85.00

Plate B-24

Top	Cuff Links	15.00-20.00
Center, Left	Cuff Links	20.00-25.00
Center	Tie Bar, Clip	25.00-35.00
Center, Right	Cuff Links	15.00-20.00
Bottom	Cuff Links	20.00-25.00

Plate B-25

Top	Cuff Links	15.00-20.00
Center	Cuff Studs	20.00-25.00
Bottom	Set: Cuff Links & Tie-Tac w/chain	10.00-15.00

Plate B-26

Top	Cuff Links	15.00-20.00
Center	Cuff Links	15.00-20.00
Bottom	Set: Cuff Links & Tie Bar	35.00-55.00

Illustrations

Plate D-1

Full Plate	Hat Ornaments	15.00-25.00

Plate D-2

Left	Hatpin	12.00-22.00
Center	Hatpin	20.00-30.00
Right	Hatpin	10.00-15.00

Plate D-3

Full Plate	Hat Ornaments	10.00-30.00

Plate D-4

Full Plate	Hat Ornaments	25.00-35.00

Plate D-5

Full Plate	Plastic Hatpins	15.00-35.00

Plate D-6

Full Plate	Hat Ornaments	10.00-35.00

Two Important Tools For The
Astute Antique Dealer, Collector and Investor

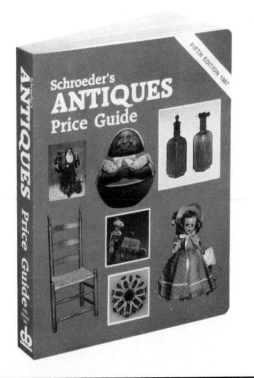

Schroeder's Antiques Price Guide

The very best low cost investment that you can make if you are really serious about antiques and collectibles is a good identification and price guide. We publish and highly recommend **Schroeder's Antiques Price Guide**. Our editors and writers are very careful to seek out and report accurate values each year. We do not simply change the values of the items each year but start anew to bring you an entirely new edition. If there are repeats, they are by chance and not by choice. Each huge edition (it weighs 3 pounds!) has over 50,000 descriptions and current values on 608 - 8½x11 pages. There are hundreds and hundreds of categories and even more illustrations. Each topic is introduced by an interesting discussion that is an education in itself. Again, no dealer, collector or investor can afford not to own this book. It is available from your favorite bookseller or antiques dealer at the low price of $11.95. If you are unable to find this price guide in your area, it's available from Collector Books, P.O. Box 3009, Paducah, KY 42001 at $11.95 plus $1.00 for postage and handling.

Flea Market Trader

Bargains are pretty hard to come by these days -- especially in the field of antiques and collectibles, and everyone knows that the most promising sources for those seldom-found under-priced treasures are flea markets. To help you recognize a bargain when you find it, you'll want a copy of the *Flea Market Trader*--the only price guide on the market that deals exclusively with all types of merchandise you'll be likely to encounter in the marketplace. It contains not only reliable pricing information, but the *Flea Market Trader* will be the first to tune you in to the market's newest collectible interests -- you will be able to buy before the market becomes established, before prices have a chance to escalate! You'll not only have the satisfaction of being first in the know, but you'll see your investments appreciate dramatically. You will love the format. Its handy 5½″x8½″ size will tuck easily into pocket or purse. Its common sense organization along with detailed index makes finding your subject a breeze. There's tons of information and hundreds of photos to aid in identification. It's written with first-hand insight and an understanding of market activities. It's reliable, informative, comprehensive; it's a bargain! From Collector Books, P.O. Box 3009 Paducah, Kentucky 42001. $8.95 plus $1.00 postage and handling.